James Joyce

Blackwell Introductions to Literature

This series sets out to provide concise and stimulating introductions to literary subjects. It offers books on major authors (from William Shakespeare to James Joyce), as well as key periods and movements (from Anglo-Saxon literature to the contemporary). Coverage is also afforded to such specific topics as 'Arthurian Romance'. While some of the volumes are classed as 'short' introductions (under 200 pages), others are slightly longer books (around 250 pages). All are written by outstanding scholars as texts to inspire newcomers and others: non-specialists wishing to revisit a topic, or general readers. The prospective overall aim is to ground and prepare students and readers of whatever kind in their pursuit of wider reading.

Shakespeare	David Bevington
Old English Literature	Daniel Donoghue
John Milton	Roy Flannagan
English Renaissance Literature	Michael Hattaway
Chaucer and the Canterbury Tales	John Hirsh
Eighteenth-Century Fiction	Thomas Keymer
American Literature and Culture 1900–1960	Gail McDonald
The Modern Novel	Jesse Matz
Old Norse-Icelandic Literature	Heather O'Donoghue
Arthurian Romance	Derek Pearsall
Mark Twain	Stephen Railton
James Joyce	Michael Seidel
Middle English	Thorlac Turville-Petre
Medieval Literature	David Wallace

James Joyce

A Short Introduction

Michael Seidel

Blackwell Publishers

Copyright © Michael Seidel 2002

The right of Michael Seidel to be identified as author of this work has been
asserted in accordance with the Copyright, Designs and Patents Act 1988.

First published 2002

2 4 6 8 10 9 7 5 3 1

Blackwell Publishers Inc.
350 Main Street
Malden, Massachusetts 02148
USA

Blackwell Publishers Ltd
108 Cowley Road
Oxford OX4 1JF
UK

Library of Congress Cataloging-in-Publication Data

Seidel, Michael, 1943–
    James Joyce, a short introduction / Michael Seidel.
        p.   cm. — (Blackwell introductions to literature)
    Includes bibliographical references and index.
    ISBN 0–631–22701–6 — ISBN 0–631–22702–4
    1. Joyce, James, 1882–1941 — Criticism and interpretation.   2. Dublin
(Ireland) — In literature.   I. Title.   II. Series.

    PR6019.O9 Z79446 2002
    823'.912—dc21

                                                            2001004355

British Library Cataloguing in Publication Data

A CIP catalogue record for this book is available from the British Library.

Typeset in 10.5 on 13 pt Meridien
by Ace Filmsetting Ltd, Frome, Somerset
Printed in Great Britain by T.J. International, Padstow, Cornwall

This book is printed on acid-free paper.

**for
Eileen**

"Sure he thinks the sun shines out of your face"
(*Exiles*, Third Act)

Contents

Abbreviations   viii

1   Introducing Joyce   1

2   Master Plots   23

3   *Dubliners*   41

4   *Portrait of the Artist as a Young Man*   59

5   *Exiles*   72

6   Levels of Narration   80

7   Homer in *Ulysses*   99

8   Three Dubliners   106

9   Reflexive Fiction   116

10 Strategic Planning   126

Notes   146

Index   153

Abbreviations

Joyce's Works

CW	*Critical Writings*, eds. Ellsworth Mason and Richard Ellmann (Ithaca: Cornell University Press, 1989).
D	*Dubliners*, with an introduction and notes by Terence Brown (New York: Penguin Books, 1992).
E	*Exiles*, introduction by Padraic Colum (New York: Viking Press,1951).
FW	*Finnegans Wake* (New York: Viking Press, 1959).
Letters	*The Letters of James Joyce*, eds. Stuart Gilbert and Richard Ellmann (3 vols. New York: Viking Press, 1957–66).
P	*Portrait of the Artist as a Young Man*, ed. with an introduction and notes by Seamus Deane (New York: Penguin Books, 1992).
Selected Letters	*Selected Joyce Letters*, ed. Richard Ellmann (New York: Viking Press, 1975).
SH	*Stephen Hero*, revised edn., eds. Theodore Spencer, John J. Slocum, and Herbert Cahoon (New York: New Directions, 1963).
U*	*Ulysses*, ed. Hans Gabler (New York: Vintage Books, 1986).

* References to individual chapters in *Ulysses* follow Joyce's lead in employing Homeric names. Chapter and line numbers are keyed to the Gabler edition.

Secondary References

Making of Ulysses	Frank Budgen, *James Joyce and the Making of Ulysses,* 2nd edn. (Bloomington and London: Indiana University Press, 1960).
Interviews and Recollections	E. H. Mikhail, ed., *James Joyce: Interviews and Recollections* (New York: St. Martin's Press, 1990).
Portraits of the Artist in Exile	Willard Potts, ed., *Portraits of the Artist in Exile: Recollections of James Joyce by Europeans* (Seattle and London: University of Washington Press, 1979).

1

Introducing Joyce

"Everything Speaks in its Own Way"

In a conversation in Paris during August of 1930 with the Czech writer Adolf Hoffmeister, Joyce described the arc of his career: "My work, from *Dubliners* on, goes in a straight line of development. It is almost indivisible, only the scale of expressiveness and writing technique rises somewhat steeply." He continues

> Each of my books is a book about Dublin. Dublin is a city of scarcely three hundred thousand population, but it has become the universal city of my work. *Dubliners* was my last look at that city. Then I looked at the people around me. *Portrait* was the picture of my spiritual self. *Ulysses* transformed individual impressions and emotions to give them general significance. "Work in Progress" [Joyce superstitiously refused to reveal the title of *Finnegans Wake* before he completed the book] has significance completely above reality; transcending humans, things, sense, and entering the realm of complete abstraction. (*Portraits of the Artist in Exile*, pp. 131–2)

My aim is to follow Joyce along the accessible arc of his career, adding commentary on his play *Exiles* and drawing from *Finnegans Wake* only as it throws light on Joyce's narrative enterprise as a whole. Joyce tells one long story, a story about the kinds of experiences the artist needs and gains in order to begin all over again to create in imaginative fullness the specific world that produced him in the first place. Joyce writes of the strains of family life in Catholic Ireland, the formation of artistic consciousness, the separation anxieties from local and familiar places, the nature of marital love, and the mythic patterns of experience recorded in world literature and re-expressed in turn-of-the-century Dublin. Characters in Joyce's works tend to migrate from one of his books to the next. That is the way he creates the feeling of a total Dublin landscape.

Joyce writes in one of the *Dubliners* stories, "The Boarding House": "Dublin is such a small city: everyone knows everyone else's business" (61). Everyone else's business becomes the stuff of Joyce's narratives – stories his father told about friends, family, and colleagues, stories local Dubliners tell about each other, whether of the tailor trying to fit a hump-backed naval captain with a new suit of clothes, or of the Irish soldier in the Crimean War who had a Russian general trained in his sights but who held fire until the general finished relieving himself on the battlefield. "Another insult to Ireland," Joyce's friend Samuel Beckett said when he heard that one.

Joyce thought of himself as a comic writer. He was the last person in the world to find his books forbidding or puzzling, and he labored under the conviction that his powers as an artist and storyteller were accessible, humane, and joyfully inspired. He never tried as a matter of course to be difficult. Rather, he had some goals in mind for what he felt narrative should and could do. A sculptor friend of Joyce's in Zurich, August Suter, asked him what of most importance had he learned from his early Jesuit schooling. Joyce's answer should encourage his readers: "to arrange things so that they can be grasped and judged" (*Portraits of the Artist in Exile*, p. 64). His arrangements ultimately required readers to readjust reading habits and techniques, but never unreasonably so. Joyce is a rational writer, and he rewards the patient and attentive reader ready to make rational sense of his works.

Of *Ulysses* Joyce said in conversation with Hoffmeister: "I don't think that the difficulties in reading it are so insurmountable. Certainly any intelligent reader can read and understand it, if he returns to the text again and again. He is setting out on an adventure with words" (*Portraits of the Artist in Exile*, p. 131). Stephen Dedalus echoes that adventure in *Portrait of the Artist as a Young Man*: "Words which he did not understand he said over and over to himself till he had learned them by heart: and through them he had glimpses of the real world about him" (64). Joyce's readers undergo the same experience and, with energy and good will, realize the same goals.

It is easy enough to say, as Joyce did, that all his work is about Dublin, but it is *about* Dublin in a way no other writer's works are. What sustains Joyce is the inventive power of his narrative language. His infatuation began early and extended into his Zurich and Paris years where friends noted how he used to sit at outdoor cafés and listen to fragments of conversation among those passing by in the streets. An American friend, Robert McAlmon, recalls speaking with Joyce.

> He was constantly leaping upon phrases and bits of slang which came naturally from my American lips, and one night, when he was slightly spiffed, he wept a bit while explaining his love or infatuation for words, mere words. Long before this explanation I had recognized that malady in him, as probably every writer has had that disease at some time or other, generally in his younger years. Joyce never recovered. (*James Joyce: Interviews and Recollections*, p. 104)

In his unfinished and abandoned autobiographical narrative, *Stephen Hero*, Joyce described himself poring over etymological dictionaries and wandering Dublin streets for unusual or rewarding words: "It was not only in Skeat that he found words for his treasure-house, he found them also at haphazard in the shops, on advertisements, in the mouths of the plodding public. He kept repeating them to himself till they lost all instantaneous meaning for him and became wonderful vocables" (30). Anything that might accrue from these wonderful vocables – from the most resonant themes in Joyce's work to the largest claims he makes about the nature of the human condition – takes second place to the pleasure and craft of formulating and reformulating words. Joyce's pacifism, his socialism, his classicism, his eurocentrism, his comic gift, his musical sensibility, his gossip-mongering, his obsession with sexuality (even deviant sexuality), his paranoia are not insignificant elements in his work; they are just secondary to the crafting, designing, manipulating, and arranging of phrases and sentences. Joyce tells Hoffmeister that by the time of *Finnegans Wake* "Each word has the charm of a living thing and each living thing is plastic" (*Portraits of the Artist in Exile*, p. 131).

Otto Luening, a young American musician and fellow student with Philip Jarnach, Joyce's duplex neighbor in Zurich during the later years of World War I, recalls Joyce in the famous Zurich cafés that at the time harbored expatriate artists, endangered politicians, and intellectuals of all stripes, including Lenin, Tristan Tzara, Hans Arp, and Ferruccio Busoni. Writers and musicians thought of themselves as craftsmen, intent on the language and media of their art. They reveled in quotation from memory or quasi-performance. A writer's or a composer's work would enter the conversation and Luening recalls how the talk would turn to reciting lines from memory or humming sections of scores and arias. On one occasion Joyce hummed the flute solo from Gluck's *Orfeo* and was so absorbed by the music that he went into a kind of trance in the middle of his rendering.[1] The raw emotion of a phrase or a sound captivated Joyce, and he could call up in the very sound of things the range of thoughts and feelings a human being could experience.

When Leopold Bloom in *Ulysses* visits the offices of the newspaper where he works, the *Freeman's Journal,* to canvas an ad, he notices the sounds of the printing press.

> Sllt. The nethermost deck of the first machine jogged forward its flyboard with sllt the first batch of quirefolded papers. Sllt. Almost human the way it sllt to call attention. Doing its level best to speak. That door too sllt creaking, asking to be shut. Everything speaks in its own way. Sllt. (7: 174–7)

Joyce creates the sound of the press, 'Sllt', and then listens as Bloom substitutes the sound the press makes for the verb 'speaks'. No writer before Joyce in prose fiction placed such priority on the structure, texture, sound, and shape of words on the page. Joyce listens to everything. In the *Dubliners* story "Ivy Day in the Committee Room," he punctuates the pompous drivel of sentimental politicians reciting an excruciatingly bad poem on Parnell with the sound of a cork popping out of a Guinness bottle: "*Pok!*" (132). Every syllable a critic. In the story "Grace," a slick-talking Irishman tumbles down a flight of barroom stairs and bites off the tip of his tongue. We see on the page what we need to know by not seeing half the words we have to imagine: "I' an't, 'an, he answered, 'y 'onge is hurt" (152).

In *Ulysses* a horse in Dublin's red light district cannot believe Leopold Bloom's phony excuse about heading home way past midnight from a neighborhood in which he has no business. Joyce gives us a horse's whinny fit for a homing epic – his version of a load of hay: "Hohohohohohoh! Hohohohome!" (15: 4879). Language and its systems are everywhere in Joyce, evoked even in toddler time early in *Portrait of the Artist* when the child tries to form the words for the song, "*O, the wild rose blossoms / On the little green place.*" The best he can do is: "*O, the green wothe botheth*" (3). When the young boy goes off to school he recalls the song and his rendition, "But you could not have a green rose. But perhaps somewhere in the world you could" (9). Joyce is perfectly aware that his reader reads the printed words, "green rose," exactly at the moment the lad wonders where in the world you could find one. Joyce's language creates the reality he represents.

Early in the day of *Ulysses*, Bloom is about to put his hat on his head. He notices that the inside band of the hat has the manufacturer's name but that the last letter is worn off. The text produces the result and a hatband speaks what Bloom sees: "Plasto's high grade ha" (4: 69). The physical look of the label produces a laugh at the silliness of it all. If the reader steps back for a moment, "high grade ha" is an even cleverer commentary on the status of Joyce's narrative as a high-grade parody (ha!) of the Homeric *Odyssey*.

Joyce's narrative at times hears before it comprehends. In the "Hades" episode of *Ulysses* the funeral carriage wheels by Farrell's statue in central Dublin. The reader experiences street sounds in the same way a figure in the carriage would – at first indistinctly and then fully formed.

> Oot: a dullgarbed old man from the curbstone tended his wares, his mouth opening: oot.
>   —Four bootlaces for a penny. (6: 229–31)

In the next chapter, "Aeolus," Joyce has Bloom watch his boss, William Brayden, editor of the *Freeman's Journal*, climb the office staircase. Bloom recalls a remark that all Brayden's brains are in the nape of his neck, then looks at the ascending hulking back as Joyce's prose images the neck in the words Bloom thinks: "Welts of flesh behind on him. Fat folds of neck, fat, neck, fat, neck" (7: 48). In "Lestrygonians," when Bloom crumples up a religious circular and flings it into the Liffey river he thinks about the law of falling bodies. Joyce has to truncate Bloom's words before gravity takes over and the circular hits the water: "thirty two feet per sec is com" (8: 57–8). A few moments later Bloom sees a woman stepping up into a tramcar and he hopes he might catch a glimpse of stocking under raised skirt: "Up with her on the car: wishwish" (8: 347–8). One compound word – "wishwish" – embodies both the sound of a swirling skirt and the nature of Bloom's desire to see under it. Later in the same chapter, Bloom steps into Davy Byrne's moral pub and Joyce produces a word for the proprietor's composite reaction:

> Davy Byrne smiledyawnednodded all in one:
> —Iiiiiichaaaaaaach! (8: 969–70)

Language is a fungible medium for Joyce and even its building blocks, the vowels, are a dominant currency in narrative exchange. Stephen Dedalus in *Ulysses* borrows a pound to spend on a prostitute from the prominent Irish revivalist poet and spiritualist, George Russell, known as A. E. He has no plans to pay it back immediately, if ever.

> A.E.I.O.U. (9: 213–13)

The vowels announcing the debt may be the closest A. E. comes to getting his money back. Joyce cannot stop laughing even into *Finnegans Wake* where the vowels transmute to a chuckle: "Ha he hi ho hu" (259), or a Shakespearean "Acomedy of Letters" (425).

"Dear, Dirty Dublin"

Joyce holds in his imagination two programs for Ireland: one, to make it a full member of the European family of nations, and two, to write its image into the literary imagination of the West. He would not trade his Irish consciousness for any other because he believed that his land had the most vital relation to language of any culture since the time of the Greeks. Yet he felt the Irish at the beginning of the twentieth century were frustrated politically by British rule, incapacitated by extremes of violence and sentiment, betrayed by internecine rivalries, and plagued by what Joyce in *Finnegans Wake* calls his countrymen's "theobibbous" allegiances to the Catholic Church and the Guinness Brewing Company.

Joyce encapsulated some of his more pronounced views on Ireland for the English lessons he used to prepare for his students at the Berlitz language school in Trieste. One vignette recorded by his pupil Alessandro Francini Bruni described the average Dubliner.

> Strictly speaking, Dubliners are my countrymen. But I don't like talking about my 'dear, dirty Dublin.' The Dubliner belongs to the race of the most vapid and inconsistent charlatans I have ever met in the island or on the continent. That's why the English Parliament has many of the biggest loud-mouths in the world.
>
> The Dubliner spends his time ceaselessly babbling in bars, pubs, and whorehouses, never tiring of the concoction which he is served and which always is made up of the same ingredients: whiskey and Home Rule. And in the evenings when he can't stand it any longer, swollen with poison like a toad, he feels his way out the door, and guided by an instinct for stability seeks out the sides of buildings, then makes his way home, rubbing his behind along all the walls and corners. He goes 'arsing along,' as we say in English. There you have the Dubliner. (*Portraits of the Artist in Exile*, p. 28)

In the midst of his struggle to publish the *Dubliners* stories, which he worked on during his early days in Trieste, Joyce needed to support himself and his family. He contributed articles to Italian newspapers and even tried his hand at a public lecture at the Università Populare in Trieste called "Ireland: Island of Saints and Sages." The lecture is crucial for understanding both Joyce's frustrations and his hopes in regard to Ireland.

> ... when the Irishman is found outside of Ireland in another environment, he very often becomes a respected man. The economic and intellectual conditions that prevail in his own country do not permit the development of individuality. The soul of the country is weakened by centuries of useless struggle and broken treaties, and individual initiative is paralysed by the influence and admonitions of the church, while its body is manacled by the police, the tax office, and the garrison. No one who has any self-respect stays in Ireland, but flees afar as though from a country that has undergone the visitation of an angered Jove. (*CW*, 171)

Irish politics provide Joyce with a theme he elaborates throughout his works: betrayal. Joyce even described to his brother Stanislaus the ritual of the mass in a nation obsessed by Catholicism as a story of betrayal, "the drama of a man who has a perilous mission to fulfill, which he must fulfill even though he knows beforehand that those nearest to his heart will betray him."[2] In his squib "Gas from a Burner," on the destruction of the sheets of *Dubliners* by a local printer upset by a few off-color words, Joyce sees himself as one of Ireland's betrayed.

> But I owe a duty to Ireland:
> I hold her honour in my hand,
> This lovely land that always sent
> Her writers and artists to banishment
> And in a spirit of Irish fun
> Betrayed her own leaders, one by one.
> (*CW*, 243)

Stephen Dedalus speaks Joyce's sentiments in *Portrait of the Artist as a Young Man.*

> —No honourable and sincere man, said Stephen, has given up to you his life and his youth and his affections from the days of Tone to those of Parnell but you sold him to the enemy or failed him in need or reviled him and left him for another. And you invite me to be one of you. I'd see you damned first. (220)

Joyce's historical prototype for Irish politics is Charles Stewart Parnell, brought down at the height of his career by the public scrutiny surrounding his adulterous affair with Kitty O'Shea, wife of a British army officer. In an essay, "The Shade of Parnell," written for a Trieste newspaper, Joyce describes Parnell as "an intellectual phenomenon,"a man of "sovereign bearing, mild and proud, silent and disconsolate" (*CW*, 226): "The melancholy which invaded his mind was perhaps the profound conviction that, in his hour of need, one of the disciples who dipped his hand in the bowl with him would betray him" (*CW*, 228). Joyce's ringing words make the point as clearly as it can be made.

> In his final desperate appeal to his countrymen, he begged them not to throw him as a sop to the English wolves howling around them. It redounds to their honour that they did not fail this appeal. They did not throw him to the English wolves; they tore him to pieces themselves. (*CW*, 228)

Joyce reprises Parnell for the *Dubliners* story that records his celebratory day in Ireland, "Ivy Day in the Committee Room." The setting is like some dark underworld zone, mediated by cold fire, where the city's deadbeats, skinflints, spoiled priests, and lost souls arrive to barter the few scraps left of local Parnell mythography. Ireland's "uncrowned king" appears again in the famous Christmas dinner sequence from *Portrait of the Artist,* one of the most evocative in all Joyce's work. The action takes place in front of a young boy, who watches and says virtually nothing as the civil strife of the nation plays out in equal doses of viciousness and crippling sentimentality: "—O, he'll remember all this when he grows up" (33), says the ardent Catholic spinster Dante Riordan, and indeed Joyce did. We read it word for word. It is hard to forget the fury of Irish self-betrayal when Dante screams at the defenders of Parnell, "—Devil out of hell! We won! We crushed him to death! Fiend!" (39). And a few lines later the demoralizing and self-pitying response of the sobbing Nationalist, Mr. Casey, "—Poor Parnell! he cried loudly. My dead king!" (39). For Stephen, as for Joyce, rank betrayal and helpless sentiment are the pit and the pendulum of Irish politics.

Another Berlitz language school vignette offers Joyce's wider perspective on Ireland.

> Ireland is a great country. They call it the Emerald Isle. The Metropolitan Government, after so many centuries of holding it by the throat, has reduced it to a specter. Now it is a briar patch. They sowed it with famine, syphilis, superstition, and alcoholism. Up sprouted Puritans, Jesuits, and bigots. (*Portraits of the Artist in Exile,* p. 27)

The potato famine of the middle decades of the nineteenth century and political manhandling by the English during the subsequent decades assured that Ireland was the only major nation in Europe to lose population during the Industrial Revolution. Joyce believed, as did most of those who pondered such matters, that a robust and expanding population was the wealth of a nation, and he bemoaned the emigration of Ireland's wild geese, her expatriates, to America, New Zealand, and Australia. He writes in "Island of Saints and Sages": "even today, the flight of the wild geese continues. Every year, Ireland, decimated as she already is, loses 60,000 of her sons. From 1850 to the present day, more than 5,000,000 emigrants have left for America, and every post brings to Ireland their inviting letters to friends and relatives at home" (*CW*, 172).

Joyce sees Ireland under triple bondage to England, to the Catholic Church, and to its own deeply factional and disastrous internal politics. He considers British rule a complex and troubled colonial relation.

> Ireland is poor because English laws ruined the country's industries, especially the wool industry, because the neglect of the English government in the years of the potato famine allowed the best of the population to die from hunger, and because under the present administration, while Ireland is losing its population and crimes are almost non-existent, the judges receive the salary of a king, and governing officials and those in public service receive huge sums for doing little or nothing. (*CW*, 167)

Joyce cannot imagine a thriving Ireland without home rule, but he was steadfastly opposed to a politics of armed rebellion and divisive confrontation. His views were identical to those expressed by Leopold Bloom in the "Eumaeus" chapter of *Ulysses*: "I resent violence and intolerance in any shape or form. It never reaches anything or stops anything" (16: 1099–1101). Joyce explained himself in a letter to his brother in terms of the policies of Arthur Griffith, the founder of the non-violent version of the *Sinn Fein* ("Ourselves Alone") movement. He approved of Griffith's approach because it favored commercial and diplomatic independence for Ireland, but he just as clearly resisted Griffith's appeal to overtly racial or nationalist hatred.

> . . . so far as my knowledge of Irish affairs goes, he [Griffith] was the first person in Ireland to revive the separatist idea on modern lines nine years ago. He wants the creation of an Irish consular service abroad, and of an Irish bank at home . . . A great deal of his programme perhaps is absurd but at least it tries to inaugurate some commercial life for Ireland and to tell you the truth once or twice in Trieste I felt myself humiliated when I heard the little Galatti girl sneering at my impoverished country. You may remember that on my arrival in Trieste I actually 'took some steps' to secure an agency for Foxford tweeds there. What I object to most of all in his paper is that it is educating the people of Ireland on the old pap of racial hatred whereas

anyone can see that if the Irish question exists, it exists for the Irish proletariat chiefly. (*Letters*, II: 167)

In *Ulysses* the narrator of the "Cyclops" episode makes fun of Bloom's politics, recalling a friend "saying it was Bloom gave the ideas for Sinn Fein to Griffith to put in his paper all kinds of jerrymandering, packed juries and swindling the taxes off of the government and appointing consuls all over the world to walk about selling Irish industries. Robbing Peter to pay Paul" (12: 1574–7). Such measures – including even a little chicanery aimed at the English – were favored ideas of Joyce's as well. Like Bloom, he preferred political, legal, and economic solutions to Ireland's problems, solutions that served national interests without encouraging national violence.

The problem for Joyce is that the nationalist ideology is an inevitably 'pigotted' (*FW*, 133) one. And the national Church is no better. Beyond its elegant rituals and ornate ceremonies, Catholicism not only placed Ireland in a subservient position to Rome but also annihilated the independent vigor of the human soul. Joyce wrote in "Island of Saints and Sages" of the possibility of Irish liberation: "But in anticipation of such a revival, I confess that I do not see what good it does to fulminate against the English tyranny while the Roman tyranny occupies the palace of the soul" (*CW*, 173). Joyce had another objection to Catholicism; he thought it the institutional enemy of modern Irish prosperity. He has Bloom make the point in *Ulysses*s: "But in the economic, not touching religion, domain the priest spells poverty" (16: 1127).

Joyce could attack Catholicism with a vengeance in his works or he could be extraordinarily funny on the subject. In the *Dubliners* story "Grace" he slaps the Church into submission by letting the self-help Catholic reformers in the story tie themselves into absurd knots over the doctrine of papal infallibility. Martin Cunningham assumes that because the pope declares infallibility at the Vatican Council of 1870, all previous popes, *ex post facto*, are retrospectively exempt from error. There are as many holes in Cunningham's argument as there are ellipses in the way Joyce presents it.

—O, of course, there were some bad lots . . . But the astonishing thing is this. Not one of them, not the biggest drunkard, nor the most . . .

out-and-out ruffian, not one of them ever preached *ex cathedra* a word
of false doctrine. Now isn't that an astonishing thing? (168)

Joyce relished mocking Church dicta, and very little struck him as
funnier than papal infallibility. When working on "Grace," he wrote
his brother Stanislaus about the 1870 Vatican Council, mimicking
the voice of the pope.

I was today in the *Biblioteca Vittorio Emanuele*, looking up the account
of the Vatican Council of 1870 which declared the infallibility of the
Pope. Had not time to finish. Before the final proclamation many of
the clerics left Rome as a protest. At the proclamation when the dogma
was read out the Pope said 'Is that all right, gents?' All the gents said
'Placet' but two said 'Non placet'. But the Pope 'You be damned!
Kissmearse! I'm infallible!' (*Letters*, II: 192)

If Joyce had a visceral distrust of radical Irish nationalists and a
spiritual distrust of the Catholic Church, he had an intellectual distrust of the Irish Revivalist movement led by W. B. Yeats, Lady
Gregory, and the poet A. E. (George Russell). The recapturing of the
Irish mythic past by the Gaelic language movement or the revival
literature of Moore and Yeats was for Joyce an impediment to cultural achievements rather than a vehicle for them. "Irish is not my
language" (189), Joyce has Gabriel Conroy say in "The Dead," echoing his own views. Joyce wrote his brother: "If the Irish programme
did not insist on the Irish language I suppose I could call myself a
nationalist. As it is, I am content to recognize myself an exile: and,
prophetically, a repudiated one" (*Letters*, II: 187).

Joyce's satiric squib "The Holy Office," set in print at his own expense but not published until he left Dublin in 1904, lists his many
quarrels with the Irish Revivalist scene and his woebegone position
within it. "The Holy Office" assumes Joyce will suffer inquisitional
review, but he directs most of his animus against the Irish Revival
writers, who are not only absurd but also driven by greed. The circle
consisting of Yeats, Lady Gregory, and A. E. are "Mammon's count-
less servitors, / Nor can they ever be exempt / From his taxation of
contempt" (*CW*, 152).

Money is at the heart of the one *Dubliners* story that presses hard-
est on Irish Revival politics, "A Mother." The story's action betrays
any nurturing satisfaction we might expect from its title. On the one

side are Mrs. Kearney and her daughter, agent and artiste performing for money, on the other, the Irish Revivalists, the something for nothing crowd. It is a bad mix. Mrs. Kearney imitates the flat accent of Mr. Fitzpatrick's appeal to the committee for authority to pay her daughter for the Revival concert: "—And who is the *Cometty*, pray?" (139). For the most part Joyce rarely provides the actual sounds of the Anglo-Irish lilt in his prose, though he does provide the locutions and rhythms. That he takes pains to do so in "A Mother" merely increases the tension that already exists in relation to what the participants think and to how they speak. Money is not the only item in dispute; so are class, culture, and language in Irish Revival politics, themes to which Joyce will return in *Portrait* and *Ulysses*.

The story depicts an investment in egos, individual and national, and its climax is a paean to mean-spiritedness, devolving into a confusion of causes and contracts, the hardening of lines over politics and finances. Joyce muddles the issue by having the young singer, Kathleen Kearney, withdraw from a performance at her mother's behest after only getting paid less than half her contracted wages. Two sentences hard upon each other embody the matter. One suggests "Mrs Kearney might have taken the *artistes* into consideration" and the other offers a stipulation of intent and value: "Pay her nothing" (146). At the end no one is right – and everyone is, if not wrong, at least discredited. The story concludes with a series of equivocal positions in parallel expressions. "I never thought you would treat us this way," says the head of the Gaelic Society, Mr. Holohan. "—And what way did you treat me?" Mrs. Kearney replies (147). "I'm not done with you," she says. "But I'm done with you," Mr. Holohan concludes (148). Joyce is done with both of them.

If Joyce is worried over the course of his career that Ireland had turned from "an intellectual force in Europe" (*CW*, 161) to a laughingstock, he still claimed in one of his Berlitz vignettes that

> Ireland, however, is still the brain of the United Kingdom. The foresighted and ponderous English provide humanity's swollen belly with the perfect instrument of comfort: the Water Closet. The Irish, doomed to express themselves in a language that is not their own, have stamped it with their genius and compete for glory with other civilized countries. This is called 'English Literature.' (*Portraits of the Artist in Exile*, p. 28)

Joyce concludes his Trieste lecture, "Island of Saints and Sages," by imagining a revival he could support, an Irish revival not unlike the one his country experienced in the latter half of the twentieth century as a republic.

> It would be interesting, but beyond the scope I have set myself to-night, to see what might be the effects on our civilization of a revival of this race. The economic effects of the appearance of a rival island near England, a bilingual, a republican, self-centred, and enterprising island with its own commercial fleet, and its own consuls in every port of the world. And the moral effects of the appearance in old Europe of the Irish artist and thinker – those strange spirits, frigid enthusiasts, sexually and artistically untaught, full of idealism and unable to yield to it, childish spirits, ingenuous and satirical, 'the love-less Irishmen', as they are called. (*CW*, 173)

Joyce's "Altar's Ego"

Among the topics that weave their way through all of Joyce's writing few are more prominent than the vocational choice Joyce makes to reject the Catholic priesthood and forge a career as an artist. In *Portrait of the Artist as a Young Man*, Stephen Dedalus frames the moment.

> All through his boyhood he had mused upon that which he had so often thought to be his destiny and when the moment had come for him to obey the call he had turned aside, obeying a wayward instinct. Now time lay between: the oils of ordination would never anoint his body. He had refused. Why? (179)

The idea of the priesthood seems to have entered Joyce's mind early, if the boy in the early *Dubliners* story "The Sisters" can in any way be said to experience the world in ways similar to the way Joyce might have experienced it. The dying spoiled priest,[3] Father Flynn, had a wish for the boy. At the center of "The Sisters" – at its crucial center – is the transmission of mystery. The priest engages the process in the only way he knows how, through those moments in the texts of his religion that he feels will speak magic to the boy, not necessarily religious magic, but the magic of accumulated knowledge, lore, tradition, ritual, mystery, and mastery. Father Flynn

had explained to me the meaning of the different ceremonies of the
Mass and of the different vestments worn by the priest. Sometimes
he had amused himself by putting difficult questions to me, asking
me what one should do in certain circumstances or whether such and
such sins were mortal or venial or only imperfections. His questions
showed me how complex and mysterious were certain institutions of
the Church which I had always regarded as the simplest acts. The
duties of the priest towards the Eucharist and towards the secrecy of
the confessional seemed so grave to me that I wondered how any-
body had ever found in himself the courage to undertake them; and I
was not surprised when he told me that the fathers of the Church had
written books as thick as the *Post Office Directory* and as closely printed
as the law notices in the newspaper. (5)

The priest's words here are of course written by a mature artist
who would eventually weave the contents of *Thom*'s (Dublin's address directory) into *Ulysses*, while making room in the "Aeolus" and
"Cyclops" episodes for sequences of raucous newspaper notices as
well. But at the time the lad listens to the priest's words he is genuine in his enthusiasm for Church doctrine and Church ritual. Yet
there is something of mockery in the story. At night the priest closes
himself in his confessional and "what do you think but there he
was, sitting up by himself in the dark in his confession-box, wide-
awake and laughing-like softly to himself" (10). The lad finally senses
a certain liberation in his death: "I felt even annoyed at discovering
in myself a sensation of freedom as if I had been freed from something by his death" (4).

Freed from what? Or Joyce might rephrase the question, freed for
what? These really are the driving questions in all Joyce's work.
Can the immense resources of tradition be brought to the fore
for something besides the repetitious and smothering business of
the Catholic Church in Ireland? Is there transference of some sort
between the religious and the artistic vocations? Stephen Dedalus
wrestles with these matters through much of Joyce's early autobiographical narrative, *Stephen Hero*, and well into the revised effort,
Portrait of the Artist as a Young Man. Joyce assumed that priests and
artists stand in something of the same mediating relation to experience. The priest officiates at the ritual that imbues material things
with spiritual value. The artist originates the process that imbues
material circumstance with aesthetic value.

Joyce made the point in a conversation with his brother: "Don't you think there is a certain resemblance between the mystery of the Mass and what I am trying to do? I mean that I am trying to give people some kind of intellectual pleasure or spiritual enjoyment by converting the bread of everyday life into something that has a permanent artistic life of its own for their mental, moral, and spiritual uplift."[4] In *Stephen Hero*, the young artist boasts, "I am a product of Catholicism; I was sold to Rome before my birth. Now I have broken my slavery but I cannot in a moment destroy every feeling in my nature" (139). Before he produces much of anything that can be called art, Stephen claims that the artist remains at the forefront of Catholicism: "The Church is made by me and my like – her services, legends, practices, paintings, music, traditions. These her artists gave her" (143). Stephen's "entire theory, in accordance with which his entire artistic life was shaped, arose most conveniently for his purpose out of the mass of Catholic theology" (205).

At a time in his life when he was confused about his vocation, Joyce was compelled by the ritual of the mass. He had no subject yet as a writer, and the mass combined form and content: "In vague sacrificial or sacramental acts alone his will seemed drawn to go forth to encounter reality: and it was partly the absence of an appointed rite which had always constrained him to inaction" (*P*, 172). But as soon as the artist seeks and finds a subject in his own life the priestly ritual loses its animating force. In *Portrait*, Stephen Dedalus takes an interest in a girl who he thinks has too intimate a friendship with a young priest: "To him she would unveil her soul's shy nakedness, to one who was but schooled in the discharging of a formal rite rather than to him, a priest of eternal imagination" (240). Even earlier, Stephen realized that ritual repetition was not art: "This was the call of life to his soul not the dull gross voice of the world of duties and despair, not the inhuman voice that had called him to the pale service of the altar" (184). Joyce fabricates a wonderful phrase in *Finnegans Wake* for the career he did not choose but that rivaled the one he did: his artist's career satisfies his "altar's ego" (463).

Beginning anew each time is what counts for Joyce. Artistic creation produces an object with its own structural and formal properties, allowing the artist the scope to experiment and expand, and, in Joyce's case, to generate from his Dublin settings the various ways language connects experience to a fuller consciousness of the race, the human race as well as the Irish race, with all its stories and myths. The artist does everything the priest does and more, reveling in confessions, not all of them benign, what *Finnegans Wake* calls those 'intimologies' (101) that make up the stuff of narrative interest. Joyce's young artist in *Stephen Hero* grasps early that "his verse allowed him to continue the offices of penitent and confessor" (32). Better yet Joyce combines the roles of the praying priest and the prying confessor in his call to artistic action in *Finnegans Wake*: "Let us pry" (188).

It is possible to trace a pattern of vocational and spiritual service in Joyce keyed to the idea of worth and obligation. Stephen has a conversation in *Stephen Hero* with a friend.

> —You want to sell your verses, don't you, said Lynch abruptly, and to a public you say you despise?
> —I do not want to sell my poetical mind to the public. I expect reward from the public for my verses because I believe my verses are to be numbered among the spiritual assets of the State. (202)

The artist undertakes a mission that undoes the damage done by the Irish priesthood – he "examines the entire community in action and reconstructs the spectacle of redemption" (*SH*, 186). Upon completing his *Dubliners* volume, Joyce insisted to his publisher, who was having cold feet about backing the stories, that "in composing my chapter of moral history in exactly the way I have composed it I have taken the first step towards the spiritual liberation of my country" (*Letters*, I: 62–3). Buck Mulligan in *Ulysses* alludes to himself and Stephen as *übermenschen* – "Toothless Kinch and I, the supermen" (1: 708–9), and Joyce may have sought support for his modernist enterprise in the great priest-baiter and moral aesthetician, Friedrich Nietzsche.

> But some time, in a stronger age than this moldy, self-doubting present, he will have to come to us, the redeeming man of great love and contempt, the creative spirit who is pushed out of any position 'outside' or 'beyond' by his surging strength again and again, whose solitude will be misunderstood by the people as though it were flight *from* reality – whereas it is just his way of being absorbed, buried and immersed in reality so that from it, when he emerges into the light again, he can return with the *redemption* of this reality.[5]

Redemptive allegory is only part of the story for Joyce or for his characters. He prefers the first phase of the mass story, the one detailing the plight of the put-upon earnest hero who returns in the latter day to avenge those who betrayed him. That hero in *Finnegans Wake* is the artist himself, "joysis crisis" (395). To see Joyce at his best and most exuberant is to watch him take the mass story through a stylistic odyssey, first in unadulterated form in Father Arnall's description of Christ's execution during the hell-fire sermon of *Portrait of the Artist*.

> He was seized and bound like a common criminal, mocked at as a fool, set aside to give place to a public robber, scourged with five thousand lashes crowned with a crown of thorns, hustled through the streets by the jewish rabble and the Roman soldiery, stripped of His garments and hanged upon a gibbet and His side was pierced with a lance and from the wounded body of Our Lord water and blood issued continually. (128)

The same story – close to the Apostles' creed – appears in an entirely different way when Stephen sees his quondam friends walk into the library in the "Scylla and Charybdis" chapter of *Ulysses*, and imagines them as a brood of mockers. He recalls the martyred Christ and plans to take artistic revenge.

> He Who Himself begot middler the Holy Ghost and Himself sent Himself, Agenbuyer, between Himself and others, Who, put upon by His fiends, stripped and whipped, was nailed like bat to barndoor, starved on crosstree, Who let Him bury, stood up, harrowed hell, fared into heaven and there these nineteen hundred years sitteth on the right hand of His Own Self but yet shall come in the latter day to doom the quick and dead when all the quick shall be dead already. (9: 493–9)

Joyce remembers Stephen's parody in the "Cyclops" episode of *Ulysses*, and applies the story yet again, but this time as a send up of the British imperial navy.

> They believe in rod, the scourger almighty, creator of hell upon earth, and in Jacky Tar, the son of a gun, who was conceived of unholy boast, born of the fighting navy, suffered under rump and dozen, was scarified, flayed and curried, yelled like bloody hell, the third day he arose again from the bed, steered into haven, sitteth on his beamend

till further orders whence he shall come to drudge for a living and be paid. (12: 1354–9)

Joyce takes extraordinary pleasure in variations on the mass story, and the malleability and comic fullness of language releases him to tell it differently each time, unlike the priest, who, as Joyce puts it in *Stephen Hero*, "must hypnotise himself every morning before the tabernacle" (139).

"Landescape"

In the spring of 1904, Joyce met and began seeing on a regular basis an eighteen-year-old young woman from Galway, then working at Finn's Hotel, Nora Barnacle. His fevered life at that time, punctuated by heavy drinking, dreadful hygienics – he rarely bathed – and bouts of despondency turned to dreams of leaving the country with Nora. This was not an easy thing to do, putting both their families on edge at the time and for years after. Many of the stories in *Dubliners* focus on the trauma of escape from Ireland and from Irish constraints upon writers. Joyce presents his first image of a bereft Irish writer in *Dubliners* when Little Chandler appears powerless and talentless: "There was no doubt about it: if you wanted to succeed you had to go away. You could do nothing in Dublin" (68). There are three local writers in the *Dubliners* stories, and each of them is paralyzed: Farrington, the professional scribe with writer's block; James Duffy, whose best effort was a manuscript translation of the play *Michael Kramer*, with a "headline of an advertisement for *Bile Beans*" (103) pasted on its first sheet; and Gabriel Conroy, a nearly anonymous reviewer for the conservative *Daily Express* given to think of himself as an "utter failure" (179).

Joyce's letter to Nora a few months before the two of them bolted to Europe, still unmarried, as they would remain officially until 1931, is telling.

I cannot enter the social order except as a vagabond. I started to study medicine three times, law once, music once. A week ago I was arranging to go away as a travelling actor. I could put no energy into the plan because you kept pulling me by the elbow. The actual difficulties of my life are incredible but I despise them. (*Letters*, II: 48)

Stephen says to his brother Maurice in *Stephen Hero*, "Isolation is the first principle of artistic economy" (33). *Finnegans Wake* calls the process 'Artalone' (418), combining in 'art' the verb and the noun. Displacement is tactical – it is time biding as the artist readies for what Joyce calls in *Finnegans Wake* "retourneys postexilic" (472). The young artist in *Portrait* uttered the mantra for those souls stifled and stymied by the culture from which they wish to draw inspiration: "silence, exile, and cunning" (269). Joyce seems to vary the mantra with the initials of his main character, HCE, in *Finnegans Wake*: "Hush, Caution, Echoland" (13). Exile for Joyce is a kind of echo land, having less to do with remove than with duplication. The artist sounds better when sounding from afar. Dedalus in *Portrait* wonders how the Irish writer will ever make something of his inchoate, violent, and sentimental land and concludes he can only manage it by taking the packet boat to Europe: "the shortest way to Tara was *via* Holyhead" (273).

Whatever Joyce's negative concerns about his homeland, though, he never abandons Ireland as an absorbing concern and as a sustaining artistic resource. He needs his land, its people, its families, its institutions, its speech rhythms, its music, its sentiments, its wit, and its memories to write. It is one of the more powerful paradoxes in Joyce's work that he sometimes says things more clearly in *Finnegans Wake* than he does elsewhere because he can get away with saying almost anything in *Finnegans Wake.* But if we listen carefully to the broken and reassembled words of that text, we can get a fairly full commentary on Joyce's habits as a writer and on his mission, even if he constantly undercuts his efforts with irony. When he says of his Europeanized writer Shem that "Shim shallave shome" (225) he means Shem shall leave home; he shall love home; and, in the end, he shall have some of whatever it is he feels he wants from home. Stephen Dedalus has a plan for artistic escape in *Portrait of the Artist*.

> —The soul is born, he said vaguely, first in those moments I told you of. It has a slow and dark birth, more mysterious than the birth of the body. When the soul of a man is born in this country there are nets flung at it to hold it back from flight. You talk to me of nationality, language, religion. I shall try to fly by those nets. (220)

Bearing the name of the most famous escape artist of myth and literature, Dedalus desires to 'fly by the nets' of his homeland. But *by* is one of those sneaky prepositions that carry antithetical meanings: *past* and *with*. Stephen means the former; Joyce invariably means both. The exilic artist, if successful, flies beyond his home but always carries it with him as an image, what Joyce, in a marvelous phrase from *Finnegans Wake*, calls "landescape" (53), the picture of the land embodied in the very action of leaving it. When Shem as penman in *Finnegans Wake* exiles himself to write in Europe he worries, comically, that he deserts his homeland. But he consistently recreates it even by trying to ignore it: "He even ran away with hunself and became a farsoonerite, saying he would far sooner muddle through the hash of lentils in Europe than meddle with Irrland's split little pea" (171). In the vernacular, the exilic artist can be said to have split the scene. And indeed, Ireland in Joyce's works is split in two, the one he remembers and the one he imagines.

In Joyce's one play, *Exiles*, the plot for a variety of reasons turns on a feature in the morning newspaper about a writer who left Ireland years before: "There is an economic and there is a spiritual exile. There are those who left her to seek the bread by which men live and there are others, nay, her most favoured children, who left her to seek in other lands that food of the spirit by which a nation of human beings is sustained in life" (99). Joyce always argued that in leaving Ireland he enabled himself to repossess it in his books. Stephen Dedalus must grasp something like this when he tells Leopold Bloom in a desultory conversation late in the day of *Ulysses* that "Ireland must be important because it belongs to me" (16: 1164–5). Bloom has no idea what Stephen is talking about, but by the time of *Finnegans Wake* Joyce converts the name of his city and the title of his own first volume of stories, *Dubliners*, into another version of belonging: "So This is Dyoublong?" (13). An artist capable of making syllables into a place *belongs* whether he stays at home or writes from abroad, "the *faubourg Saint Patrice* called Ireland for short" (*U*, 16: 1161–2).

Joyce's friend Philippe Soupault noted of Joyce that "each day, and each hour of the day, he thought of Ireland; he lived and relived his memories; thousands of times he mentally traversed the streets and squares of the city." Soupault asked why Joyce refused to return and his "elongated hand stirred, like a blind man, the pages he was writing at that time" (*Portraits of the Artist in Exile*, p. 116). Joyce makes an early stab at defining the artistic process in *Stephen Hero* and he comes very close to defining the necessary exilic process as well, the doubling that ensues from recreating a remembered place. Stephen imagines the artist

> standing in the position of mediator between the world of his experi-
> ence and the world of his dreams – a mediator, consequently gifted
> with twin faculties, a selective faculty and a reproductive faculty. To
> equate these faculties was the secret of artistic success: the artist who
> could disentangle the subtle soul of the image from its mesh of defin-
> ing circumstances and most exactly re-embody it in artistic circum-
> stances chosen as the most exact for it in its new office, he was the
> supreme artist. (77–8)

For Joyce, who effectively left Ireland for good in 1904, returning only for three brief visits, the supreme artist lives on in local time abroad, and "beats" time only the way a musician might at the po-dium.

> *Your genus its worldwide, your spacest sublime!*
> *But, Holy Saltmartin, why can't you beat time?*
>   (*FW*, 419)

2

Master Plots

Life Between Kicksheets

Joyce told a friend, Georges Borach, that "there are indeed hardly more than a dozen original themes in world literature" (*Portraits of the Artist in Exile,* p. 71), all touching on an individual's bonds and obligations, on love inside the family and out, and on where one presumes to go when one leaves home. In and around these themes, Joyce recycles concerns of special importance to him: Who are the artist's rivals and what are the artist's impediments? What is it to be touched by the creative muse? What do characters give or give up to get what they feel they want? Joyce sees all stories participating together in a master plot for narrative, a natural plot that traces experience from birth to death as a series of egresses and re-entries, "the lingo gasped between kicksheets" (*FW,* 116), birth bed, death bed, and "allaphbed" (*FW,* 18).

To one degree or another, all narrative is based on different ratios of estrangement and reconciliation. Stephen Dedalus understands the process when he says not once but twice during his analysis of Shakespeare in *Ulysses,* "—There can be no reconciliation, Stephen said, if there has not been a sundering" (9: 397–8). Later he thinks about the octave that replicates in musical terms life's basic plot: "the fundamental and the dominant are separated by the greatest possible interval which . . . [is] the greatest possible ellipse. Consistent with. The ultimate return. The octave" (15: 2105–12).

Thresholds within that master plot present narrative opportunities for all writers, and especially for Joyce. Inertia or paralysis is the first threshold. The next is the threshold of escape. The final threshold is *nostos* or homecoming. Joyce's first three finished books correspond to each threshold. *Dubliners* focuses on those who are stuck in a place or condition in which their potential as human beings, as lovers, as artists is stifled. *Portrait* tracks the most fabulous escape story of mythical history, Daedalus out of the Cretan labyrinth. *Ulysses* adapts for modern times the return of a versatile, all-round man to his tarnished home. The homecoming plot offers Joyce his greatest challenges – betrayal, usurpation, conspiracy, alienation of affections – but also his greatest satisfactions. A hero can return to his doom, as in the Agamemnon story, or to fulfillment as in the *Odyssey*. Joyce's favorite opera, Puccini's *Madama Butterfly*, presents a third possibility, what Stephen Dedalus might call "almosting it" (*U*, 3: 366–7). The most poignant aria in the score, "*Un bel di vedremo*" ("One fine day he will return"), tries to coax a proper homecoming out of a plot that has other intentions. Butterfly's aria moved Joyce to tears. She sees a wisp of white smoke from the steamer in the harbor and assumes Lieutenant Pinkerton has returned to her as promised: "You see? He's come! . . . I shall go to the top of the hill and wait, but I won't mind this long waiting . . . All this will happen, I promise you." It does not.

Epic Consciousness

One of Joyce's most clearly stated goals is to present his city to a community of readers. He writes to his brother before the publication of *Dubliners*: "When you remember that Dublin has been a capital for thousands of years, that it is the 'second' city of the British empire, that it is nearly three times as big as Venice it seems strange that no artist has given it to the world" (*Letters*, II: 111). Joyce's imagination always traveled well beyond the confines of the Dublin he planned to give to the world. His scope was epic in the sense of fullness, or what Renaissance writers called *copia*, an expansion of narrative design to allow works to sum up and recapitulate what has gone before. Joyce was not the first artist, nor would he be the last, to build his own work upon the foundations of others. At the time he was working on the *Dubliners* stories in Trieste, Joyce delivered his public lecture on Ireland, arguing that "the Irish nation's insistence on developing its own culture by itself is not so much the demand of a young nation that wants to make good in the European concert as the demand of a very old nation to renew under new forms the glories of a past civilization" (*CW*, 157). Ireland awaits its epic awakening, and Joyce announces the need for a new national bard.

> The old national soul that spoke during the centuries through the mouths of fabulous seers, wandering minstrels, and Jacobite poets disappeared from the world with the death of James Clarence Mangan. With him, the long tradition of the triple order of the old Celtic bards ended; and today other bards, animated by other ideas, have the cry.
>
>   One thing alone seems clear to me. It is well past time for Ireland to have done once and for all with failure. If she is truly capable of reviving, let her awake, or let her cover up her head and lie down decently in her grave forever. (*CW*, 173–4)

Joyce's *Finnegans Wake* bears a title that allows the Irish hero to awaken so that he might participate in the very "wake" that was supposed to have finished him off. In *Ulysses*, the proto-bard Stephen Dedalus hears the Irish Revivalists plan a meeting that night – to which he is not invited – by lamenting that "Our national epic has yet to be written" (9: 309). Joyce thinks himself the man for the job, and he thinks *Dubliners*, *Portrait of the Artist*, and *Ulysses* the first installments on the plan. *Finnegans Wake* would follow. The Irish epic that Joyce writes invites the rest of the world in. There is no action or plot that he can construct that does not belong in some real sense to plots that retroactively make up those stored in the warehouse of world literature. "It is all so often and still the same to me" (625), Joyce writes in *Finnegans Wake*, all "The seim anew" (215). The phrase carries within it four keywords for what Joycean narrative can do: *seme* (seed or originate); *seem* (imitate); *same* (repeat); *seam* (connect). Dare Joyce also mean, "See him" anew, as he did in *Ulysses* when he made Leopold Bloom Homer's Odysseus?

"Ere we are!" (599), Joyce writes in *Finnegans Wake*, and the range of his vision extends to the past "ere," the present "here," and the local "Eire" or Ireland. In a paper he read on "Drama and Life" at the age of twenty for presentation at Dublin's University College Literary and Historical Society, Joyce argued that the rudiments of an epic age may be gone, but the limitless scope of the "great human comedy" is still available for the artist.

Epic savagery is rendered impossible by vigilant policing, chivalry has
been killed by the fashion oracles of the boulevards. There is no clank
of mail, no halo about gallantry, no hat-sweeping, no roystering! The
traditions of romance are upheld only in Bohemia. Still I think out of
the dreary sameness of existence, a measure of dramatic life may be
drawn. Even the most commonplace, the deadest among the living,
may play a part in a great drama. It is a sinful foolishness to sigh back
for the good old times, to feed the hunger of us with the cold stones
they afford. Life we must accept as we see it before our eyes, men and
women as we meet them in the real world, not as we apprehend
them in the world of faery. The great human comedy in which each
has share, gives limitless scope to the true artist, to-day as yesterday
and as in years gone. (*CW*, 45)

Joyce believes that literature, somewhat like the universe itself, is
infinitely collapsible and expandable. He writes of "adamelegy" (77)
in *Finnegans Wake*, the process by which the whole story of the race
from origins (Adam) to ends (elegy) plays out as "etymology." In an
early essay, "The Study of Languages," Joyce argued, "in the history
of words there is much that indicates the history of men" (*CW*, 28).
Consciousness begins with the word and then expands outward to
the wider world. As a youngster at Clongowes Wood College, Stephen
writes on the flyleaf of his geography book what Joyce, in effect,
does in all his fiction – expand boundaries from individual to uni-
versal, from local to cosmic.

> *Stephen Dedalus*
> *Class of Elements*
> *Clongowes Wood College*
> *Sallins*
> *County Kildare*
> *Ireland*
> *Europe*
> *The World*
> *The Universe* (12)

Stephen's analysis of Shakespeare in *Ulysses* makes the same point:
the stuff of drama and narrative re-creates the imagining mind as it
expands its boundaries and plots adventures.

He found in the world without as actual what was in his world within as possible. Maeterlinck says: *If Socrates leaves his house today he will find the sage seated on his doorstep. If Judas go forth tonight it is to Judas his steps will tend*. Every life is many days, day after day. We walk through ourselves, meeting robbers, ghosts, giants, old men, young men, wives, widows, brothers-in-love, but always meeting ourselves. (9: 1041–6)

In a passage from later in the day, the narrator of "Ithaca" takes Bloom where the epic has a desire to go by projecting his itinerary eastwards and westwards. In other words, the passage connects Joyce's modern epic to its roots and expands its world westward to newer and more modern shores. Bloom in his dreams will pass through

Ceylon (with spicegardens supplying tea to Thomas Kernan, agent for Pulbrook, Robertson and Co, 2 Mincing Lane, London, E. C., 5 Dame street, Dublin), Jerusalem, the holy city (with mosque of Omar and gate of Damascus, goal of aspiration), the straits of Gibraltar (the unique birthplace of Marion Tweedy), the Parthenon (containing statues of nude Grecian divinities), the Wall street money market (which controlled international finance), the Plaza de Toros at la Linea, Spain (where O'Hara of the Camerons had slain the bull), Niagara (over which no human being had passed with impunity), the land of the Eskimos (eaters of soap), the forbidden country of Thibet (from which no traveller returns), the bay of Naples (to see which was to die), the Dead Sea. (17: 1980–90)

Does Bloom stop here at the Dead Sea, where one would think life itself stops? Joyce has another surprise in store for the modern Odysseus and the modern comic epic. He takes Bloom to regions of wider compass than any epic traveler before.

Ever he would wander, selfcompelled, to the extreme limit of his cometary orbit, beyond the fixed stars and variable suns and telescopic planets, astronomical waifs and strays, to the extreme boundary of space, passing from land to land, among peoples, amid events. Somewhere imperceptibly he would hear and somehow reluctantly, suncompelled, obey the summons of recall. Whence, disappearing from the constellation of the Northern Crown he would somehow reappear reborn above delta in the constellation of Cassiopeia and after incalculable eons of peregrination return an estranged avenger,

a wreaker of justice on malefactors, a dark crusader, a sleeper awakened, with financial resources (by supposition) surpassing those of
Rothschild or the silver king.   (17: 2013–23)

Comic Temperament

To mark the temperament of an artist is to observe his resting place
at the end of works. Joyce's endings suggest movement but they do
not define its significance in any absolute sense. At the end of the
day in *Ulysses* the narrative asks of Leopold and Molly Bloom in bed:
"In what state of rest or motion?" (17: 2306).

> At rest relatively to themselves and to each other. In motion being
> each and both carried westward, forward and rereward respectively,
> by the proper perpetual motion of the earth through everchanging
> tracks of neverchanging space. (17: 2307–10)

Joyce never assumes that any action settles a life conclusively,
perhaps because most of his individual stories and at least two of his
longer narratives comprise but one day in representational time. Of
all his finished works, only *Portrait of the Artist as a Young Man* and
several stories from *Dubliners* ("The Boarding House," "A Painful
Case," "A Mother," and "Grace") break beyond the scope of a day or
evening. While each moment in a life brings an immense amount to
bear on every thought and every action, the next day offers a different dispensation. Comedy is the genre of second chances; tragedy
the genre of ended motions. Joyce is more interested in stories of
revival than of foreclosure.[1] He even attributed his fame to two books,
one that ends with sleep and another that begins with the word
"wake" in its title: "fame would come to you twixt a sleep and a
wake" (*FW*, 192). Leopold Bloom in the funeral chapter of *Ulysses*
says, "Read your own obituary notice they say you live longer. Gives
you second wind. New lease of life" (6: 795–6). Bloom may not
know it, but his very words describe his status as Odysseus renewed
in Dublin. Joyce's works are filled with the dead awakened in every
conceivable form, from the buried Paddy Dignam revived in the
"Cyclops" episode of *Ulysses* to proclaim the great conveniences of
astral culture: "tālāfānā, ālāvātār, hātākāldā, wātāklāsāt" (12: 345), to

Tim Finnegan, who jumps out of his coffin to join the party because everyone is having such fun at *Finnegans Wake*.

As a rule, Joyce reacts negatively to the despair associated with tragic form. Those works in which the focus is unremittingly on failure limit the joy Joyce associated with literature, a joy to which he was partial because he saw the word in the first letters of his name. Too many die in tragedy, and those who survive are miserable. Joyce offers a cryptic commentary on the Shakespearean tragedies, especially *Hamlet*, when he has Stephen make fun of Trinity Professor Edward Dowden's populist view of Shakespeare, "William Shakespeare and company, limited" (*U*, 9: 729). The tragic question from *Hamlet*, "To be or not to be, that is the question," becomes for Joyce the comic answer: "To me or not to me. Satis thy quest on" (*FW*, 269).

Satisfaction is a key literary ingredient for Joyce. His young writer in *Stephen Hero* gravitates towards an artistic "temper of security and satisfaction and patience" (78), an attribute of classical form in which "the sane and joyful spirit issues forth and achieves imperishable perfection, nature assisting with her goodwill and thanks" (78–9). For Joyce, "the feeling which is proper to comic art is the feeling of joy" ("Paris Notebook," *CW*, 144). When Bloom crawls into bed with his wife at the end of *Ulysses* after ruminating on the entire day, the narrative asks the key question: "In what final satisfaction did these antagonist sentiments and reflections, reduced to their simplest forms, converge?" (17: 2227–8), and the answer is the rounded action of a day and the ample form of a warm body.

> Satisfaction at the ubiquity in eastern and western terrestrial hemispheres, in all habitable lands and islands explored or unexplored (the land of the midnight sun, the islands of the blessed, the isles of Greece, the land of promise), of adipose anterior and posterior female hemispheres, redolent of milk and honey and of excretory sanguine and seminal warmth, reminiscent of secular families of curves of amplitude, insusceptible of moods of impression or of contrarieties of expression, expressive of mute immutable mature animality. (17: 2229–36)

Stephen Dedalus makes one of the few direct references to the actual classical character, Ulysses, upon whom Joyce based his day of his novel when he explains why he prefers Shakespearean romance to Shakespearean tragedy.

—If you want to know what are the events which cast their shadow over the hell of time of *King Lear, Othello, Hamlet, Troilus and Cressida*, look to see when and how the shadow lifts. What softens the heart of a man, shipwrecked in storms dire, Tried, like another Ulysses, Pericles, prince of Tyre? (*U*, 9: 400–4)

Stephen prefers the late romances because they imbue life with hope.

—Marina, Stephen said, a child of storm, Miranda, a wonder, Perdita, that which was lost. What was lost is given back to him: his daughter's child. *My dearest wife*, Pericles says, *was like this maid*. Will any man love the daughter if he has not loved the mother? (9: 421–4)

What was lost and returned in Shakespearean late romance was "A child, a girl" (9: 406), placed in the satisfied hero's arms. Joyce always had a notion that a child instills a kind of special hope in individuals and in a race of individuals. The death of a child for the Blooms in *Ulysses* is one of the paralytic memories of the book, and the possibility of another may be one of the motivations for both Leopold and Molly to rekindle their married life in a productive way. Bloom considers the matter: "No son. Rudy. Too late now. Or if not? If not? If still?" (11: 1067). And Joyce sums up the hope of continuity and comedy in two of the few crystal clear sentences he writes in *Finnegans Wake*, about the myth of Tara and the special hero-children of the race: "Or see only a youth in his florizel, a boy in innocence, peeling a twig, a child beside a weenywhite steed. The child we all love to place our hope in for ever" (621).

"Speak Clothse to a Girl's"

Joyce said that *Ulysses* was, among other things, the epic of the human body, but when he describes Stephen Dedalus as Telemachus in the schematic note sheets provided for the book's first translators and critics, he writes, "Telemachus has no body."[2] There is a clue, though, how the young artist might find one. In the schema for Stephen's chapters, he noted: "Penelope (Muse)." There is no Penelope, strictly, in Stephen's chapters, but for Leopold Bloom's wanderings Joyce lists "Penelope (wife)." Around Dublin, Bloom's wife is known as "Madam Bloom, the vocal muse" (7: 609).

As the day develops in *Ulysses* it becomes clear that Stephen will not meet Molly Bloom, though very late at night he sees the light of her presence from the reflection of a lamp in her window. Stephen soon walks into the dark of that early morning never to be seen again in Joyce's fiction, and Joyce emerges at a later date to write the books that bring him to June 16, 1904, the date on which he sets *Ulysses*. That is also the date on which Joyce first stepped out on an evening stroll with Nora Barnacle, the woman he was to spend the next thirty-six years of his life with in several European cities. The young artist leaves Joyce's fictional scene on the very day that the more mature author's muse arrives. It is no secret that Joyce held in almost mystical awe the inspiring power of his own relationship with Nora.[3] He saw his love as comparable to a kind of religious intensity, and refers to it with the same language he reserves for art. One of his evenings with Nora in Dublin before they left for Europe appeared as "a kind of sacrament and the recollection of it fills me with amazed joy" (*Letters*, II: 49). Later, in 1909, he writes Nora passionately after a disturbing rift in their relationship.

> Guide me, my saint, my angel. Lead me forward. *Everything* that is noble and exalted and deep and true and moving in what I write comes, I believe, from you. O take me into your soul of souls and then I will become indeed the poet of my race. I feel this, Nora, as I write it. My body soon will penetrate into yours, O that my soul could too! O that I could nestle in your womb like a child born of your flesh and blood, be fed by your blood, sleep in the warm secret gloom of your body! (*Selected Letters*, 169)

Joyce listened to Nora by the hour that he might hear in the otherness of a woman's voice the contents of the feminine psyche and the speech patterns he could transfer to his own work. A young girl asks the putative artist in *Finnegans Wake*, "Did you really never in all our cantalang lives speak clothse to a girl's before?" (148). When Joyce feels himself most inspired his writing actually does "speak clothse" to a girl. Mangan's sister, whose name connects her to one of Joyce's favored Irish poets, James Clarence Mangan, appears in the *Dubliners* story "Araby" and stirs the blood of desire and imagination in the young boy: "I had never spoken to her, except for a few casual words, and yet her name was like a summons to all my foolish blood" (22). The sight of her is an inspiration.

Or if Mangan's sister came out on the doorstep to call her brother in to
his tea we watched her from our shadow peer up and down the street.
We waited to see whether she would remain or go in and, if she remained, we left our shadow and walked up to Mangan's steps resign-
edly. She was waiting for us, her figure defined by the light from the
half-opened door. Her brother always teased her before he obeyed and
I stood by the railings looking at her. Her dress swung as she moved
her body and the soft rope of her hair tossed from side to side. (22)

When Joyce told his brother Stanislaus that there was warmth
and beauty in his stories even if one had to scour the pages of *Dubliners* to find any, he directed him to the passage of the harpist and
his harp from "Two Gallants" where muse and music conspire.

Not far from the porch of the club a harpist stood in the roadway,
playing to a little ring of listeners. He plucked at the wires heedlessly,
glancing quickly from time to time at the face of each new-comer and
from time to time, wearily also, at the sky. His harp too, heedless that
her coverings had fallen about her knees, seemed weary alike of the
eyes of strangers and of her master's hands. One hand played in the
bass the melody of *Silent, O Moyle*, while the other hand careered in
the treble after each group of notes. The notes of the air throbbed
deep and full. (48)

Even daughter Polly, the bait in the con game of "The Boarding
House," is a sight to behold: "She wore a loose open combing-jacket
of printed flannel. Her white instep shone in the opening of her
furry slippers and the blood glowed warmly behind her perfumed
skin. From her hands and wrists too as she lit and steadied her can-
dle a faint perfume arose" (62). When Gretta Conroy in "The Dead"
appears on the stairs she provides the entire volume an appropriate
muse, a woman from the shadows or one of the most beautiful of
the living dead. Gabriel Conroy watches as the sound of music accompanies the image.

He stood still in the gloom of the hall, trying to catch the air that the
voice was singing and gazing up at his wife. There was grace and
mystery in her attitude as if she were a symbol of something. He asked
himself what is a woman standing on the stairs in the shadow, listening to distant music, a symbol of. If he were a painter he would paint
her in that attitude. Her blue felt hat would show off the bronze of

her hair against the darkness and the dark panels of her skirt would show off the light ones. *Distant Music* he would call the picture if he were a painter. (211)

Gabriel remembers the image when he thinks of a phrase in a letter he wrote Gretta many years before: "Is it because there is no word tender enough to be your name?" (215). Joyce continues: "Like distant music[4] these words that he had written years before were borne toward him from the past" (215), and the muse does what the muse almost always does in Joyce, turns inspiration into desire: "Perhaps she would not hear at once: she would be undressing. Then something in his voice would strike her. She would turn and look at him" (215). We see the feminine muse in *Finnegans Wake*, and her name is literally a pun on help: "But there's a little lady waiting and her name is A.L.P." (102).[5] For Joyce, "The word is my Wife" (167). As the chapter in the *Wake* that critiques the books puts it: "Who in his heart doubts either that the facts of feminine clothiering are there all the time or that the feminine fiction, stranger than the facts, is there also at the same time, only a little to the rere?" (109).[6] A little to the "rere" has its evocative qualities, but so much the better. Writing has a body to it, and inspiration is a natural process as even Stephen sensed in *Portrait*: "In the virgin womb of the imagination the word was made flesh" (236).

Where does this leave Stephen whose pain is "not yet the pain of love" (*U*, 1: 102)? Stephen says to Cranly, thinking of his own flame, Emma, in *Stephen Hero*, "You're incomplete without a woman" (215), and late in the day of *Ulysses*, in the "Circe" episode, Bloom seems intent on believing that his new young friend Dedalus calls out for his girlfriend, even though what Bloom hears are a few lines from Yeats' poem, "Who Goes with Fergus": "Ferguson, I think I caught. A girl. Some girl. Best thing could happen him" (15: 4950–1).

Without love for Joyce there is little joy, sustenance, desire, or energy. "What is the word known to all men?" (3: 435), Stephen asks walking along the strand in *Ulysses*. Joyce answers in *Finnegans Wake*: "O love it is the commonknounest thing" (269), the most common noun and the most commonly known one. At the end of *Portrait*, Stephen guesses that the act of love and the act of writing are similar: "I desire to press in my arms the loveliness which has not yet come into the world" (273). Joyce sets a series of kisses given or not given, withheld or given under duress as the test in *Portrait* for Stephen's inspirational capacity: "—Tell us, Dedalus, do you kiss your mother before you go to bed?" (10) asks his young schoolmate Wells. The question is bound to get Stephen in trouble no matter how he answers it, and, indeed, that is Wells' intent. Stephen suffers not simply a rhetorical confusion, but embarrassment: "Was it right to kiss his mother or wrong to kiss his mother?" (11). Is the kiss a gesture of sustenance, inspiration, love, or is it incestuous, vampiric, threatening, paralyzing? One of Stephen's many problems in *Portrait* is that he has too little love to give and readies himself to shun that which he gets. He freezes on the tram step with E. C. at Harold's Cross.

> —She too wants me to catch hold of her, he thought. That's why she came with me to the tram. I could easily catch hold of her when she comes up to my step: nobody is looking. I could hold her and kiss her.
>   But he did neither.(73)

The kiss not taken on the tram turns up in a poem Stephen writes to honor the very occasion he thwarted: "when the moment of farewell had come the kiss, which had been withheld by one, was given by both" (74). He signs the poem with the Jesuit motto, L.D.S. (*Laus Deo Semper* or Praise to God Always), and Joyce would like his reader to keep that motto in mind when an older Stephen sees his "strange and beautiful seabird" of a girl, with her slender legs and her "thighs, fuller and softhued as ivory, . . . bared almost to the hips where the white fringes of her drawers were like featherings of soft white down" (185). Stephen's "Heavenly God!" (186) at that moment addresses his poetic hormones more than his poetic theology. He virtually signs the bird-girl epiphany as he signed the poem, though a moment of sheer sexual and artistic inspiration replaces a Jesuit reflex.

Late in *Portrait* Stephen hears his rustic friend Davin's story about the peasant woman luring him into her cottage—"a type of her race and his own, a batlike soul waking to the consciousness of itself in darkness and secrecy and loneliness and, through the eyes and voice and gesture of a woman without guile, calling the stranger to her bed" (198). When he thinks again of Davin's story of the peasant cottager, he reacts: "But him no woman's eyes had wooed" (259). He thinks of E. C. in the same way, first as a child "that she had worn a shawl about her head like a cowl and that her dark eyes had

invited and unnerved him" (87) and then as a "figure of the woman-
hood of her country, a batlike soul waking to the consciousness of
itself" (239–40). By then he was in the middle of writing another
poem to E. C., a villanelle dealing with the relationship between li-
bido and creation. In *Ulysses* Stephen is still uncertain what the love of
a woman means or whether it is the love of the right woman. Of
Shakespeare he says, "He was chosen, it seems to me. If others have
their will Ann hath a way. By cock, she was to blame. She put the
comether on him" (9: 256–7). But as he works out the sequence of
Shakespeare's artistic life in the chapter it becomes clear that Ann
Hathaway was at the center of all plots that gave Shakespeare his
poetic and dramatic sustenance. Stephen then asks the same question
of himself he had framed in *Portrait*, "Who will woo you?" (9: 938).
Earlier he had scribbled a few verses about a vampiric kiss on a piece
of paper torn from Mr. Deasy's letter on infectious cattle disease.

> *On swift sail flaming*
> *From storm and south*
> *He comes, pale vampire,*
> *Mouth to my mouth.*
>   (7: 522–5)

The vampiric kiss is an infection. *Ulysses* offers an alternative kiss as
Leopold Bloom recalls the day on Howth when he proposed to Molly.
The muse is there, only a little to the rere.

> High on Ben Howth rhododendrons a nannygoat walking surefooted,
> dropping currants. Screened under ferns she laughed warmfolded.
> Wildly I lay on her, kissed her: eyes, her lips, her stretched neck beat-
> ing, woman's breasts full in her blouse of nun's veiling, fat nipples
> upright. Hot I tongued her. She kissed me. I was kissed. All yielding
> she tossed my hair. Kissed, she kissed me. (8: 911–16)

This is more like it.

"All This Way to Show Us a French Triangle"

There is a curious moment in *Ulysses* when Stephen Dedalus agrees
to try to help his employer, Mr. Deasy, get a letter on foot and mouth

disease, then plaguing Ireland's livestock, published in one of Dublin's newspapers. He thinks that if he does, his roommate and rival, Buck Mulligan, will make him pay: "Mulligan will dub me a new name: the bullockbefriending bard" (2: 430–1). But how would Mulligan know unless Stephen told him? The nature of rivalry is one of the more potent and vexed themes in all Joyce's work. One assumes Joyce sets up patterns of rivalry because a fair or even unfair fight is always a good story. Joyce, though, has other reasons. Rivals are less antagonists for Joyce than stimulants. Stephen will tell Mulligan about the foot and mouth letter because the witty abuse he plans to receive will challenge him and, in a strange way, satisfy him.

Exaggerated or exacerbated rivalry initiates action and energizes characters. No Joyce plot is complete unless he inserts a rival – dead or alive – into the mix. Gabriel Conroy in "The Dead" feels bested by a boy who died years before in Galway. Stephen Dedalus and Father Moran compete for the attention of E. C. in *Portrait* and the result is a love poem tainted with revenge. Two writers – Robert, a journalist, and Richard, a novelist – contest in *Exiles* for the novelist's common-law wife; two proto-writers, Mulligan and Stephen, and two commercial men, Boylan a promoter and Bloom an ad man, contest in *Ulysses* for what amounts to the home space. In *Finnegans Wake*, Shem calls his twin brother Shaun "his polar andthisishis" (177).

The rival desires what his other wants. In each of these instances Joyce complicates the plot by a kind of willful complicity. In the original version of the Stephen–Father Moran rivalry from the early *Stephen Hero*, we read this bit of intriguing text.

> Stephen watching this young priest and Emma together usually worked himself into a state of unsettled rage. It was not so much that he suffered personally as that the spectacle seemed to him typical of Irish ineffectualness. (66)

Stephen needs Emma and her priest to focus his estrangement in Ireland. The two attend Gaelic League meetings, a double dose of ignominy for Stephen, who sees Emma's priestly dalliance and the Gaelic that binds it as a betrayal not only of his friendship but also of the English language in which he writes. Of course, when he writes his poem in *Portrait* he concludes: "his anger was also a form of homage" (239). Stephen makes something of the same point in his complex argument in the Library chapter of *Ulysses* about the supposed infidelity of Shakespeare's wife Ann Hathaway, which releases Shakespeare as a writer as much as it agonizes him as a man. One of Stephen's auditors in the library concludes, "You have brought us all this way to show us a French triangle" (9: 1064–5). All of Joyce's important works do the same. The French triangle is a mediated love relation in which desire is sustained by allowing, even encouraging, a third party in a love relation. The ensuing opportunity is one of the key lessons of *Finnegans Wake*: "Problem ye ferst, construct ann aquilittoral dryankle Probe loom!" (286). And the book does, based on the physical look of Anna Livia Plurabelle's body.

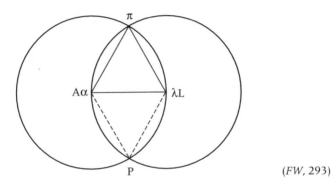

(*FW*, 293)

Joyce calls his triangle "Vieus Von DvbLIn" (293): "This it is an her. You see her it" (298). Joyce imagines the rival lovers, who are also twins and brothers (representing all men), in a relation with their mother (representing all women), the artist twin taking the front view, the other the rear: "You, allus for the kunst and me for omething with a handel to it" (295).

Why is the triangular relation so important to Joyce that he reconfigured the entire plot of the *Odyssey* to present a faithless Penelope in the figure of Molly Bloom engaging in an afternoon affair with a man who may be friendlier with her husband than either of them admits? One answer touches upon the mystical bond between a man and a woman that Joyce saw as defined less by the sexual constraints of marital convention than by free choices made over and over.[7] In *Exiles* Richard has a discussion with his child Archie about what can be taken by others and what cannot. He says it is much better to give because then no one can take anything from you: "It is yours then for ever when you have given it. It will be yours always. That is to give" (47).

For Joyce triangular desire is the gift that keeps on giving. Nora confided to a friend of the Joyces, Frank Budgen, that "Jim wanted her to go with other men so that he would have something to write about."[8] One of Budgen's friends, the Swiss sculptor August Suter, made the same point, though more discreetly.

> In Zurich Joyce had introduced his wife to Greeks and Jews, models for Bloom, and apparently would have liked, with a touch of curiosity, to see his wife discomposed. Mrs. Joyce realized that he was playing with her virtue, and refrained from thus serving as a model for her husband's books. (*Portraits of the Artist in Exile*, p. 64)

Bloom's ideas in *Ulysses* may not stray far from Joyce's own. In the "Circe" episode, Joyce represents every private thought a character ever had as if the entire public is in on it. A mock-trial puts Bloom next to a woman he does not know but whom he might have seen stepping up on a tram earlier that day: "He urged me (stating that he felt it his mission in life to urge me) to defile the marriage bed, to commit adultery at the earliest possible opportunity" (15: 1054–6). In *Exiles*, Richard Rowan simply admits to the man trying to sleep that night with his wife: "I longed to be betrayed by you and by her – in the dark, in the night – secretly, meanly, craftily. By you, my best friend, and by her. I longed for that passionately and ignobly, to be dishonoured for ever in love and in lust . . ." (70). He says to his wife about the man who either seduced her or spent most of the night trying, "I cannot hate him since his arms have been around you. You have drawn us near together" (75).

Joyce told Budgen that *Ulysses* offered a version of the adultery plot in which the bourgeois husband winks because, for one or another reason, it suits him to count on the sexual distraction of his wife by a lover (*Making of Ulysses*, p. 314). The French have an entire genre of jokes based on the cuckolded husband intruding on his wife and her lover, politely apologizing for the inconvenience and telling both to "*continuez.*" Adultery is the least of it in Joyce's wilder imagination. Robert McAlmon remembers a conversation with Joyce in which the two of them "talked of the way the free mind can understand the possibility of all things: necrophilia and other weird rites" (*Interviews and Recollections*, p. 104), and then recalls Nora saying, "I guess the man's a genius, but what a dirty mind he has, hasn't he?" (p. 106).

Before considering Joyce's ideas too strange, it pays to recall a remark of Richard's in *Exiles*: "Many ideas strike a man who has lived nine years with a woman" (42). The problem for Joyce and for his characters in triangle plots is that the ratio of stimulation to jealousy is not exactly predictable. More to the point, there is no telling what the threat or even the suggestion of infidelity will do to a relationship. Jealousy is not an easy subject for Joyce. In his calmer intellectual moments he downplayed its place in the artistic temperament, relegating it to the tortuous paths of tragedy, the debilitating violence of *Carmen* or the murderous design of *Othello*, where, as Stephen Dedalus puts it of Shakespeare, "His unremitting intellect is the hornmad Iago ceaselessly willing that the moor in him shall suffer" (9: 1023–4).

When fidelity, or Joyce's idea of it, was most dramatically tested with Nora, Joyce became nearly inconsolable, not only in terms of what he imagined Nora *might* do with others, but also in terms of what he imagined she had *already* done. For years he brooded over the competition for Nora's favors with his friend Vincent Cosgrave before he left with Nora for Europe in the winter of 1904, and, like Gabriel Conroy in "The Dead," he remained gallingly convinced that the young tubercular boy so taken with Nora in Galway, Michael Bodkin, was her real and ardent lover. An exchange of letters in 1909 between Joyce, in Dublin for a visit, and Nora, still in Trieste, was so charged that the letters were exempted from the collected edition until Richard Ellmann published those not lost or destroyed in 1975. Joyce recalls the young boy from Galway, who was the model for Michael Furey in the *Dubliners* story, and we can see him negotiate the terrain between jealousy and excitement.

Did that boy you were fond of ever do it? Tell me now, Nora, truth for truth, honesty for honesty. When you were with him in the dark at night did your fingers *never, never* unbutton his trousers and slip inside like mice? . . . Darling, darling, tonight I have such a wild lust for your body that if you were here beside me and even if you told me

with your own lips that half the redheaded louts in the county Galway had had a fuck at you before me I would still rush at you with
desire. (*Selected Letters*, p. 183)

Writing *Exiles* and recasting the fidelity theme of the *Odyssey* into a
French triangle in *Ulysses* may have been Joyce's way, in part, of
dissipating the jealousy he felt in his own life and turning it towards
erotic, more productive, more satisfying, more artistic ends. When
Robert in *Exiles* explains his desire for Richard's wife, Bertha, "No
man ever yet lived on this earth who did not long to possess – I
mean to possess in the flesh – the woman whom he loves. It is nature's law" (63), Richard responds that there is something that transcends possessive jealousy. Robert asks what, and Richard says, "To
wish her well" (63). Bertha's response to Robert's advances is exactly what Richard desires, if it were possible to mute his jealousy:
"Still I was excited, of course. But not like with you, Dick" (49).
Molly Bloom might – and in her way does – say the same thing
about her day with Blazes Boylan and her earlier life with Bloom.
For Joyce, to license a rival just to the point that he can still be
subsumed is to wish one's self well.

3

Dubliners

"There Was no Hope for Him This Time"

On the day Joyce sets *Ulysses*, June 16, 1904, Stephen quits his job teaching youngsters at a day school because he claims he was not born to be a teacher, but "—A learner rather" (2: 403). An hour and a half later he finds himself in the newspaper offices of the *Freeman's Journal* angling to tell a story he has put together from bits and fragments of events occurring during that very day. Just before he proceeds he gives himself something of a pep talk: "Dublin. I have much, much to learn" (7: 915). "—I have a vision too, Stephen said" (7: 917), and then he thinks to himself, "Dubliners" (7: 922): "On now. Dare it. Let there be life" (7: 930). The story he tells is about two old Dublin vestals who climb Nelson's Pillar in the heart of the Hibernian metropolis and drop plum pits on passers-by below. This is the presumptive state of Dublin, and the two vestals turn soon enough into the two sisters of the opening story of *Dubliners*, "The Sisters."[1]

Joyce had tried to escape Dublin late in 1902 to pursue a course of medical studies in Paris, but he returned in April of 1903 when his father sent him a telegram that his mother was near death. The telegram was mangled in transmission and came out, "nother dying, come home father," which Joyce thought summed up the condition in Ireland at large. Joyce remained in Dublin for the next year and a half trying to support himself as a reviewer, an essayist, a musician, and even, possibly, an actor. He began writing short stories with the intent of selling them one at a time and then shaping them into a volume for publication.[2] With his family life deteriorating rapidly and with his father drinking and on a downward financial spiral, Joyce had to make some decisions. For one, he escaped the immediate confines of his family, which he did by taking up temporary residence with a friend, Oliver St. John Gogarty, in one of the Martello towers built by the British along the Irish coast.

In June of 1904, Joyce met the great love of his life, Nora Barnacle, and several months later he tried to convince her to leave Ireland with him for good. He wrote to her in mid-September and what he said holds for every story in the *Dubliners* collection, stories on which he was working at the time: "There is no life here – no naturalness or honesty. People live together in the same houses all their lives and at the end they are as far apart as ever" (*Letters*, II: 53). Joyce also wrote Nora about what awaited her if she ran off to Europe with the reprobate he pictured himself to be. In trying to shield her from the worst, he described his relation to the city and nation that had produced him. To think of home is to stare a corpse in the face, and that is exactly why he begins the first story of *Dubliners* with the dead body of a paralytic Irish priest. To Nora, he puts it this way.

> My mind rejects the whole present social order and Christianity – home, the recognized virtues, classes of life, and religious doctrines. How could I like the idea of home? My home was simply a middle-class affair ruined by spendthrift habits which I have inherited. My mother was slowly killed, I think, by my father's ill treatment, by years of trouble, and by my cynical frankness of conduct. When I looked on her face as she lay in her coffin – a face grey and wasted with cancer – I understood that I was looking on the face of a victim and I cursed the system which had made her a victim. (*Letters*, II: 48)

The first sentence of *Dubliners* is a striking one: "There was no hope for him this time" (1). Nominally, it describes the old, dying priest, but if readers take the opening of "The Sisters" with some degree of seriousness, then *Dubliners* is Joyce's doomsday book. His opening sentence echoes the famous inscription over the gates of hell in Dante's *Inferno*: LASCIATE OGNE SPERANZA VOI CH'INTRATE or "Abandon hope all ye who enter."[3] All that is vibrant in Dublin suffers enervation, paralysis, exhaustion.

Joyce was somewhat worried about the tone of the stories. He wrote a letter to his brother Stanislaus from Trieste in September

1906 about wanting to do better with the *Dubliners* collection. He wished to say something about Ireland that he felt was missing in the volume, something genuine about his land's musical soul, about its warmth, its grace, and its extraordinary hospitality.

> Sometimes thinking of Ireland it seems to me that I have been un-necessarily harsh. I have reproduced (in *Dubliners* at least) none of the attraction of the city for I have never felt at my ease in any city since I left it except in Paris. I have not reproduced its ingenuous insularity and its hospitality. The latter 'virtue' so far as I can see does not exist elsewhere in Europe. I have not been just to its beauty: for it is more beautiful naturally in my opinion than what I have seen of England, Switzerland, France, Austria or Italy. And yet I know how useless these reflections are. (*Letters*, II: 166)

When Joyce's first publisher, Grant Richards, began to balk at some of the harsh language in the volume, Joyce expanded upon the description of what he was trying to do and how he was trying to do it. One of his great subjects is buried in this simple description. In every piece of narrative he produces he strives for age-appropriate consciousness.

> My intention was to write a chapter of the moral history of my country and I chose Dublin for the scene because that city seemed to me the centre of paralysis.[4] I have tried to present it to the indifferent public under four of its aspects: childhood, adolescence, maturity and public life. The stories are arranged in this order. I have written it for the most part in a style of scrupulous meanness and with the conviction that he is a very bold man who dares to alter in the presentment, still more to deform, whatever he has seen and heard. I cannot do any more than this. I cannot alter what I have written. (*Letters*, II: 134)

One phrase from the Richards letter – "scrupulous meanness" – needs a bit of unpacking. Joyce did not want to suggest by the phrase mean-spirited. He meant precise. Part of the pleasure in reading Joyce is to come upon passages that are *mean* only in light of their near perfection of detail. Here, for example, is the first extended look we get at a character in the volume, the priest Father Flynn, a figure of repulsive fascination for the young boy narrating the story, who has a hunger for the kind of things the priest knows without the pitfalls of the kind of thing the priest is.

Perhaps my aunt would have given me a packet of High Toast for him and this present would have roused him from his stupefied doze. It was always I who emptied the packet into his black snuff-box for his hands trembled too much to allow him to do this without spilling half the snuff about the floor. Even as he raised his large trembling hand to his nose little clouds of smoke dribbled through his fingers over the front of his coat. It may have been these constant showers of snuff which gave his ancient priestly garments their green faded look for the red handkerchief, blackened, as it always was, with the snuff-stains of a week, with which he tried to brush away the fallen grains, was quite inefficacious. (4)

Keywords

The young boy of "The Sisters" connects his fascination with the dying body of the priest to three words, words that seem to hold for him some mystical or maleficent significance: paralysis, gnomon, and simony. These words that so fascinate the lad control the structure of Joyce's entire collection of stories, and the words carry over into the design of large elements of *Portrait of the Artist, Exiles, Ulysses,* and *Finnegans Wake* as well.

> Every night as I gazed up at the window I said softly to myself the word *paralysis*. It had always sounded strangely in my ears, like the word *gnomon* in the Euclid and the word *simony* in the Catechism. (1)

Paralysis

Paralysis rivets Joyce because so much in his psyche and his aesthetics is based on its opposite, on movement – intellectual, emotional, physical movement out of Ireland. Stephen Dedalus thinks about history in the "Nestor" chapter of *Ulysses*, and concludes with Aristotle that "It must be a movement then, an actuality of the possible as possible" (2: 67). No one ever moves in the stories, with the exception of the European drivers in "After the Race" and the journalist Gallaher in "A Little Cloud" (and to them good riddance). The starkest image of paralysis in the volume occurs in the figure of the paralytic priest in the first story, and Joyce reflects that image in his Trieste lecture on Ireland. He writes that in his homeland "initiative is paralysed" (*CW*, 171), and only the "old men, the corrupt, the children, and the poor stay at home, where the double yoke wears another groove in the tamed neck; and around the death bed where the poor, anaemic, almost lifeless, body lies in agony, the rulers give orders and the priests administer last rites" (*CW*, 172).

The *Dubliners* stories present one vivid scene after another replicating the thematic paralysis Joyce sees in his city, from the distraught lad at the end of "Araby" to the young girl in "Eveline" who seems frozen at the pier while the ship that would take her to South America boxes the compass in the harbor.

> —Come!
> No! No! No! It was impossible. Her hands clutched the iron in frenzy. Amid the seas she sent a cry of anguish!
> —Eveline! Evvy!
> He rushed beyond the barrier and called to her to follow. He was shouted at to go on but he still called to her. She set her white face to him, passive, like a helpless animal. Her eyes gave him no sign of love or farewell or recognition. (34)

At the time Joyce was working on the early *Dubliners* stories he was also sketching out his autobiographical novel *Stephen Hero*, and as his young man wandered the streets of Dublin he elaborated the image Joyce had already identified as endemic in his land.

> These wanderings filled him with deep-seated anger and whenever he encountered a burly black-vested priest taking a stroll of pleasant inspection through these warrens full of swarming and cringing believers he cursed the farce of Irish Catholicism: an island [whereof] the inhabitants of which entrust their wills and minds to others that they may ensure for themselves a life of spiritual paralysis. (146)

Gnomon

Gnomon means the shape of a smaller parallelogram taken away from a larger one, a missing piece or ghost of a form not quite there. The concept controls much of *Dubliners* and much of Joyce's notion of realistic narrative generally, in that life offers very few instances in which resolute meaning comes into definitive focus. "No, not tell all" (11: 876), thinks Leopold Bloom at one point during the day of

Ulysses, and he could not have better described the principle of the gnomon in Joyce's work. Coming to terms with the missing is as important as comprehending the present. When some of the *Dubliners* stories are told over again in *Ulysses* – Bob Doran's story, Tom Kernan's story, possibly even James Duffy's story – new material enters in. As one of young Stephen Dedalus' class-mates at Clongowes puts it in *Portrait of the Artist* about the ways to frame a riddle on his name, Athy (a thigh), "—There is another way but I won't tell you what it is" (24). We never know the precise moment Stephen rejects the priesthood in *Portrait.* We never know what Beatrice and Robert do during their tryst in *Exiles.* We never know what Bloom buries about his complicity in his wife's adultery in *Ulysses.* And who is the mysterious bloke in the mackintosh who shows up at the funeral during the day of *Ulysses?*[5] What happened with Dedalus and his friends at the Westland Row train station late at night in *Ulysses* before the visit to the red light district? And just what did Earwicker, the pubkeeper, do in Phoenix Park in *Finnegans Wake* that has almost everyone in the book so agitated?

As for *Dubliners,* each story in the volume is a gnomon or has one.[6] There is a missing piece of information, an event not entirely explained, an image that does not appear whole, an explanation that is incomplete. The central missing piece of "The Sisters," the history and circumstances of the old priest, manifests as he laughs to himself hidden inside his empty confession box at night – he is not quite all there. Joyce reinforces the technical sense of the gnomon in "The Sisters" by forming one sentence after another around its verbal equivalent, the ellipsis, where the sentence itself has a missing part. The boy in relation to Mr. Cotter is in much the same position as the reader is to the story. He "puzzled my head to extract meaning from his unfinished sentences" (3).

> —No, I wouldn't say he was exactly . . . but there was something queer . . . there was something uncanny about him. I'll tell you my opinion . . . (1)

Much else is missing in the stories. What exactly is the "old josser" doing in the middle of the empty field near the Dodder river in "An Encounter"? What kind of scam operation is at work in "After the Race"? What happened before "Two Gallants" begins and what happens at its end precisely? What does Polly think about in "The Boarding House"? Where are the missing years of "A Painful Case"? What goes on in the Halloween game in "Clay"? What is the shady incident in the pub at the beginning of "Grace" all about? What happens at the very end of "The Dead"?

One of the best illustrations in *Dubliners* of the principle in action occurs in "Clay." Failure for Ireland in the story is an accumulation of small things left out – a missing plum cake, a deleted stanza of a ballad – and the primary character is a small, left-out thing herself. Maria is innocent, gentle, but flustered, ineffectual, and essentially unconscious. She has no life, really; she exists as a point of mediation in a world that has nothing left to mediate. The whole of the action turns sad, sour, and vulgar when the children slip a lump of clay – or something more vile, according to the shrewd critic and reader, Margot Norris – into the dish at a traditional All Soul's Day party game. If Norris is right, the title word – a symbol of death in the game – does not even make it into the story.

The last great, symphonic story in the volume, "The Dead," is gnomonic to the core. Gabriel Conroy misses something in almost everything. He comments ironically early in the evening on what Joyce plans for him, though Gabriel will never grasp the whole of it: "I think we're in for a night of it" (177). To Lily, Gabriel wonders out loud whether she plans to return to school. She says not this year or any more, for that matter. Gabriel makes a gesture at understanding what she might mean, but obviously gets it wrong: "—O, then, said Gabriel gaily, I suppose we'll be going to your wedding one of these fine days with your young man, eh?" (177). Her reply stuns him: "The girl glanced back at him over her shoulder and said with great bitterness: —The men that is now is only all palaver and what they can get out of you" (178). It is almost as if Lily has another story to tell – though she will not tell it – and that Gabriel has touched a raw nerve. Perhaps Lily is in a condition that Gabriel's question could not possibly have intended her to reveal. Gabriel's response is an awkward offer of a seasonal gratuity, which covers over the animus of Lily's outburst.

Joyce sets Gabriel up for what will happen again – he stumbles upon a missing segment of his wife's life: "—Tell me what it is, Gretta. I think I know what is the matter. Do I know?" (219). He does not. It is important to realize that Gabriel does nothing grotesquely wrong, which adds to the story's power in revealing how life's disappointments are a collection of minor gnomons, minimal transgressions, frustrations, and inadequacies real or imagined, with the addendum that those who imagine themselves inadequate usually are. Gabriel never quite gets it, and thinks of his wife what Joyce sees as inevitable in life: "Perhaps she had not told him all the story" (223).

Simony

Simony has a precise meaning in religious contexts, the material debasement of spiritual values, adapted from the name Simon Magus, the Samaritan sorcerer who tried to buy the apostles' "tricks" in the New Testament. But Joyce employs simony for all acts of devaluation, religious or secular. In *Stephen Hero*, the young autobiographical artist says: "Simony is monstrous because it revolts our notion of what is humanly possible" (203). All the spoiled priests, mocking artists, boasters, besters, and braggadocios of Joyce's world are simoniacs, including Simon Dedalus of *Portrait* and *Ulysses*. Simony is ungenerous in spirit, corrupt and corrupting, humanely debasing. Joyce explains something of the tone he tries to sound in *Dubliners* when he writes to his prospective publisher about the collection: "I think people might be willing to pay for the special odour of corruption which, I hope, floats over my stories" (*Letters*, II: 123).

Acts of simony often center on the perversion or bartering of love. "Two Gallants" presents a scene in which love is bought and sold either too cheap or too dear by a pair of down-at-the-heel Dublin succubae. The structure of the story is about killing time while the action that signifies – the wresting of money from a young Dublin servant – takes place just beyond the range of the narrative map. We can venture guesses as to both motive and result – the two scoundrels extort money from a young woman – but we cannot be absolutely sure how they set the scheme up or whose money they get, the girl's or her employer's. What we can know is that we have experienced a violation. The unexplained action is, in this instance, literally an act of simony: taking money for matters of the heart.

Title Words

If Joyce begins *Dubliners* with a series of words whose meanings can generate plots, he does not stop with the ones on the first page of "The Sisters." Many of the title words of the stories do similar work. "An Encounter" is an early story that marks in its title a number of uncomfortable and unproductive encounters represented in the course of all the stories: Jimmy's scamming by the euro-playboys in "After the Race," Corley plying the slavey in "Two Gallants," Bob Doran succumbing to Polly in "The Boarding House," Farrington countering whomever he meets in "Counterparts," Mr. Duffy and Mrs. Sinico in "A Painful Case," Mrs. Kearney and Mr. Holohan in "A Mother," Mr. Kernan and the Catholic Church in "Grace."

One of the worst encounters of all takes place on a field abutting the Dodder river in Dublin. Two young boys cut school for an adventure. At one point they pass by the "Vitriol Works" (14) without realizing that what they have in store for them is much worse. "An Encounter" offers the first narrative test of domestic adventure in *Dubliners*. Stimulants to the imagination for the young are wild, exotic, and remote – the American west of "An Encounter," the alluring bazaar of "Araby," the distant Buenos Aires of "Eveline." In all cases the residue of adventure is stagnation. The youngsters of "An Encounter" do not need or want the stimulation the story offers – in fact they seem not to want much at all, suffering from the same velleity as Ireland: "It was too late and they were too tired" (16). A seedy stranger accosts them on an empty field near the river – "a queer old josser" (18) – who first tantalizes the boys with formulaic comments about young girls and then performs some kind of act in the middle of the field, never quite described: "—I say! Look what he's doing!" (18). The man returns to the lads to begin fetishizing about child whipping. At the conclusion of the story we have a debased and sorry version of a lad enacting the Irish game of rebellion, and he is, irony of ironies, almost alone (*sinn fein*) after the tale's encounter.

The title "Araby" names both a bazaar in Sandymount and the locus of unrealized desire for a young boy depressed by the drab streets of an impoverished and declining city. The boy wishes to visit "Araby" to purchase a gift for Mangan's sister, though the gift he would truly like to give her is a gift she would never receive: himself.

At the end the dreariness of the bazaar and its smarmy occupants cancels the grace and beauty of the image of Mangan's sister in the boy's imagination. The moment is a bad encounter – experience dashes the poignancy of expectation. The lad calls his reaction vanity because desire has turned to dust. Vanity is the only word he knows – a reflex of his Catholicism – though vanity is not the right word. Deflated is much better. The end of the story makes more sense when readers know that the only important name in it, Mangan, is the name of a poet, James Clarence Mangan, whom Joyce revered and about whom he spoke in 1902 to the Literary and Historical Society of Dublin's University College. At the end of "Araby" the young boy is in the grips of a kind of Catholic sorrow imagined in the Mangan essay as one of the problems of Irish sentiment and self-pity: "All his poetry remembers wrong and suffering and the aspiration of one who has suffered and who is moved to great cries and gestures when that sorrowful hour rushes upon the heart" (*CW*, 80).

"Counterparts" is another title word so strong in its structural implications that Joyce could well have used it to title *Dubliners* as a whole. Each substantial figure in the volume has a counterpart somewhere else, an opposite, a double, or a ghost. The two sisters at the beginning balance the two Morkan sisters at the end. Father Flynn in his coffin from the first story returns after a fashion with the monks who sleep in their coffins from "The Dead." The mothers, Mrs. Mooney in "The Boarding House" and Mrs. Kearney in "A Mother," share particularly rapacious qualities. Little Chandler at the end of "A Little Cloud" finds his anti-soulmate in Farrington at home at the end of "Counterparts." The vision of Mangan's sister from "Araby" reappears as a vision of Gretta Conroy on the stairs from "The Dead." Gabriel Conroy faces a counterpart of himself when he stares in the mirror at the end of the story and sees

> himself as a ludicrous figure, acting as a pennyboy for his aunts, a nervous well-meaning sentimentalist, orating to vulgarians and idealising his own clownish lusts, the pitiable fatuous fellow he had caught a glimpse of in the mirror. (221)

"Grace" is a title word that catches the double yoke, religious and secular, worn around the necks of most Dubliners. Joyce is crafty in using religious terminology to juxtapose a Catholic-obsessed culture with the ironies of behavior exhibited in it. *Grace* means religious absolution and election, or a period of allowance and license, or a kind of personal bearing. Each of these is at issue in the story "Grace" in a series of comic ways, the object of which is to make a "new man" of the Protestant Tom Kernan by replacing the gracelessness with which he fell down a flight of stairs at the beginning with the grace of muscular Catholicism at the end.

Even though not a title word, the word "reparation" works in similar fashion in "The Boarding House." "Reparation" directs two plot lines. In a religious sense, reparation makes the soul whole while absolving sin. All life is in a way reparation for original sin, and Bob Doran, recognizing Catholic good works over faith, has no recourse but to pay reparations over and over for falling victim to the whims of sexual desire: "The instinct of the celibate warned him to hold back. But the sin was there; even his sense of honour told him that reparation must be made for such a sin" (62). In a legal sense, reparation repairs damage to person or property, and Mrs. Mooney plays both of those secular trumps when she dangles her daughter as sexual lure. We know exactly what to expect of her actions, and the story delivers. "The Boarding House" is Dickensian in its judgments, and Joyce writes of Mrs. Mooney, the butcher's wife, that she "dealt with moral problems as a cleaver deals with meat" (58). Doran's fate is sealed when he gave in to desire and faced the pressure of reparation, for him a kind of blood sacrifice. Mr. Doran "had a notion he was being had" (61). More often than not Joyce suspends his characters' judgments on such matters. They are "had" without necessarily feeling it. The story ends with reparation as marriage sacrament, Doran's unuttered proposal to Polly.

—Come down, dear. Mr. Doran wants to speak to you.
Then she remembered what she had been waiting for. (64)

"The Dead" as a title word serves as the volume's shroud. Joyce's brother Stanislaus wrote him in 1905 that he had heard an Irish baritone at a concert sing the song from Moore's collection, "Irish Melodies." Joyce asked his brother to send the lyrics. "You move like men who live," the song intones, and Joyce drew from that image not only the conception for his final story, but certification for the dead, material and spiritual, who haunt and even mock all the stories in *Dubliners*. In "The Sisters," the lad thinks, "The fancy came to me that the old priest was smiling as he lay there in his coffin" (6). "Araby" begins with a description of a dead-end Dublin street, a blind, and one of the first things we learn in the story is that the "former tenant of our house, a priest, had died in the back draw-ing-room" (21). "DEATH OF A LADY AT SYDNEY PARADE" (109) reads the paragraph in the *Dublin Daily Express* in "A Painful Case." The sentimentalized ghost of a dead Parnell haunts "Ivy Day in the Committee Room." The offhand palaver at the Morkans' annual Christmas dinner dance in "The Dead" picks up the title word – the "three mortal hours" (176) it takes Gretta to dress, the cold that must make her feel "perished alive" (177), Michael Furey's singing that "would get his death in the rain" (223). Gabriel notices above the piano a picture of the "two murdered princes in the Tower" (186) from Shakespeare's *Richard III*. The dinner conversation turns to dead opera singers, and a few lines from an exquisite ballad of a dead baby sung by Bartell D'Arcy recalls for Gretta Conroy the dead boy, Michael Furey, from the gasworks of Galway. *Dubliners* begins with a dying priest laid out as a corpse in his coffin and ends with a blanket of white spread over the whole land. "He had a beautiful death" (7) says one of the sisters of her brother in the first story of the volume, "The Sisters," and in the last paragraph of the last story of *Dubliners* we get a description – at least on a verbally symbolic level – of a truly beautiful death, what Joyce in *Finnegans Wake* will call "house of the gonemost west" (66).

Earlier in the story, Miss Ivors taunted Gabriel about a trip to the western isles and Gabriel thinks himself bullied when his wife chimes in, "—O, do go, Gabriel, she cried. I'd love to see Galway" (191). Little did he know at that point how significant a memorial trip back to Galway will be for him, though Joyce certainly did. The kernel of the story had obviously been with him for years and stayed with him after the writing. In September of 1909, two years after com-pleting "The Dead," and after rekindling yet again the memory of Michael Bodkin (Michael Furey) who forms the basis of the story, Joyce wrote his wife, Nora: "You will not quarrel with me any more, will you, dear? You will keep my love always alive. I am tired to-night, my dearest, and I would like to sleep in your arms, not to do anything to you but just to sleep, sleep, sleep in your arms" (*Selected Letters*, p. 169).

When at the end the story sets off into inarticulateness – which at its simplest level may merely be sleep – distinctions are no longer clearly made between Dublin's living and dead, her waking and sleeping souls. Perhaps Joyce provides a clue about the ending of the story in a letter he wrote Nora even before he left with her for Europe.

> It seems to me that I am always in your company under every possible variety of circumstances talking to you walking with you meeting you suddenly in different places until I am beginning to wonder if my spirit takes leave of my body in sleep and goes to see you. (*Letters*, II: 46)

The evocative ending of "The Dead" makes sense in the context Joyce develops for it over the years.

> The time had come for him to set out on his journey westward. Yes, the newspapers were right: snow was general all over Ireland. It was falling on every part of the dark central plain, on the treeless hills, falling softly upon the Bog of Allen and, farther westward, softly falling into the dark mutinous Shannon waves. It was falling, too, upon every part of the lonely churchyard on the hill where Michael Furey lay buried. It lay thickly drifted on the crooked crosses and headstones, on the spears of the little gate, on the barren thorns. His soul swooned slowly as he heard the snow falling faintly through the universe and faintly falling, like the descent of their last end, upon all the living and the dead.[7] (225)

Narrative Experiments

Each *Dubliner* story sets its own tone and deals with its own particular issues, but there are moments in the volume where Joyce begins to approach techniques he developed and employed with far greater persistence in later works. "Eveline" is a case in point. The story begins with Eveline framed at her window. She may never escape that frame, immobilized and paralyzed at beginning and at end. Joyce first published "Eveline" in the very month that he and Nora planned their escape from Dublin, so in some sense he must have understood the difficulty of the decision for Eveline and even the odds against her making it.[8] He wrote Nora in September of 1904:

> I intended to tell you that if you receive the least hint of any act on
> the part of your people you must leave the Hotel at once and send a
> telegram to me (at *this* address) to say where I can see you. Your
> people cannot of course prevent you from going if you wish but they
> can make things unpleasant for you. (*Letters*, II: 55)

For risk-takers familiarity breeds contempt; for the fearful it promises comfort. "Eveline" is grudging in the extreme – everything about
it. Even Eveline's choice of words in glossing over her time at home
with a difficult father, "she did not find it a wholly undesirable life"
(31), takes as much as it gives. The original printings of the story
produced an ellipsis (another gnomon) just before the final paragraph, indicating either a break in time or possibly in voice. The last
paragraph may in fact be a projection of Eveline's immobile consciousness, not the actual event at the dock railing but a projection
inside her head of what the day of departure would be like should
she even be capable of standing at the pier. Eveline's paralysis seems
to root her to the windowsill where the story began. If she truly
never left the windowsill and her narrative consciousness produces
the scene, then Joyce begins to experiment with the extraordinary
inventiveness he displays in *Ulysses* when, with subtle keying techniques, he moves inside characters' heads to produce internal versions of scenes that may or may not actually take place.

In another early *Dubliners* story, "Two Gallants," readers experience a version of Joyce's drop-in realism that they will see again in
large doses in *Ulysses,* most notably at the end of the "Oxen of the
Sun" chapter where half a dozen speaking voices overlap with no
attempt on the part of the narrator to identify them other than by
linguistic idioms and clues. "Two Gallants" is a version of this technique in more explicable form – readers join the elliptical conversation of two Dublin gadabouts who know more about each other and
about what they are doing than the reader ever will know. The effect is almost akin to eavesdropping. Conversations take place with
little explanation in regard to local idioms or private information.

> —Well! . . . That takes the biscuit!
>   His voice seemed winnowed of vigour; and to enforce his words he
> added with humour:
>   —That takes the solitary, unique, and, if I may so call it, *recherché*
> biscuit! (44)

Readers are never told what, in any language, takes the biscuit. Many of Joyce's epiphanies are little more than snippets of conversation with no more context than what those who overhear can make of them. He had described the technique at length in *Stephen Hero*:

> The Young Lady—(drawing discreetly) . . . O, yes . . .
> I was . . . at the . . . cha . . . pel . . .
>   The Young Gentleman—(inaudibly) . . . I . . . (again inaudibly) . . .
> I . . .
>   The Young Lady—(softly) . . . O . . .but you're . . . ve . . . ry . . .wick
> . . .ed . . .
>   This triviality made him think of collecting many such moments together in a book of epiphanies . . . He believed that it was for the man of letters to record these epiphanies with extreme care, seeing that they themselves are the most delicate and evanescent of moments. (211)

Joyce in these instances feels himself under no obligation as a storyteller to tell readers why his characters speak the way they do, exactly what they mean, why they do not always finish sentences, why they use idiomatic words and expressions. One of the more startling features of his narrative realism is that it resists aiding a reader by something so obvious as an explanation. It is not as if Joyce knows these things and simply will not reveal them; rather, he tries to mimic in narrative representation the phenomena that normal people experience a dozen times during the course of a day.

"A Painful Case" is the first of Joyce's works to experiment with a series of techniques that become extremely important later in *Portrait*, *Ulysses*, and *Finnegans Wake*. The story begins by playing a subtle reflexive game with narrative voices, and then moves on to bigger things. Joyce intends his character James Duffy to be off-putting, so he finds the perfect image for the man in the narrative tics that make him up. Duffy "had an odd autobiographical habit which led him to compose in his mind from time to time a short sentence about himself containing a subject in the third person and a predicate in the past tense" (104). To reinforce the manner in which style manifests as content, Joyce ends the story with a paragraph of eight sentences, each of which exhibits the very narrative habit that separates Duffy from his own self.

He turned back the way he had come, the rhythm of the engine pounding in his ears. He began to doubt the reality of what memory told him. He halted under a tree and allowed the rhythm to die away. He could not feel her near him in the darkness nor her voice touch his ear. He waited for some minutes listening. He could hear nothing: the night was perfectly silent. He listened again: perfectly silent. He felt that he was alone. (113–14)

Near the conclusion of the story Joyce introduces a technique that might be called stylistic layering, one in which he folds other kinds of written material into the body of his text. He will do this extensively in later works, from the completely cribbed hell-fire sermon in *Portrait of the Artist* to the encyclopedic inclusion of the day's print venues into *Ulysses* to radio shows and street ballads in *Finnegans Wake*. In "A Painful Case" Joyce includes a printed version of a newspaper account of the death of Mrs. Sinico inside the exterior narrative, and inside the newspaper account he includes snippets from a coroner's report. In effect, we have three stylistic versions of the action occurring at the same time: the version extended over several years that the main narrative provides, that which a reporter might glean from a few hours on the scene, and that which a coroner records for an official inquest. The main narrative seems to lose four years in three words: "Four years passed" (108). The reporter loses Duffy. The coroner loses the living Mrs. Sinico – he merely reads the corpse, which is the way that *Dubliners* began in the first place with Father Flynn in his coffin.

The process is ingenious. A secondary narrative, enfolded as a newspaper article, bears as its subtitle the same phrase as the narrative that surrounds it: "A Painful Case." A series of phrases from the news account and the coroner's report provide a contrapuntal understanding of the action of the entire story. While nominally describing Mrs. Sinico's death as "sudden failure of the heart's action" (110), the coroner hits on Mr. Duffy's symbolic failing. At the moment of Mrs. Sinico's touch earlier in the story, James Duffy's heart failed him. At the end of the news account, the coroner's words undercut the action of the whole: "No blame attached to anyone" (111). The point of the story is that blame, for one reason or another, attaches to everyone.

Other phrases from the enfolded material haunt the story and engage its action. A drunken Mrs. Sinico was done in by the engine of the slow train "while attempting to cross the line" (109). That is precisely what she did when she precipitously and, it turned out, disastrously, reached out to Mr. Duffy: "one night during which she had shown every sign of unusual excitement, Mrs Sinico caught up his hand passionately and pressed it to her cheek" (107). The trainman in the news account broke the forward movement of his engine and "brought it to rest in response to loud cries" (110). Mrs. Sinico's whole being is a *cri de coeur*. A witness faces an investigator's question: "You saw the lady fall?" (110). Well, so did we as readers, though the fall came earlier than the one that kills her. Another witness discovers Mrs. Sinico "apparently dead" (110). That sums up for Joyce's readers the condition of many Dubliners in all the stories. We learn that her "injuries were not sufficient to have caused death in a normal person" (110), but we also know that part of her abnormality can be laid at the feet of Mr. Duffy.[9] The railway officials are exempted from negligence "in view of certain other circumstances" (110), circumstances that make up the bulk of the story we have just read. Mrs. Sinico's husband testifies that "his wife began to be rather intemperate in her habits" (111). He means alcohol; we as readers know that her intemperate habits concerned Mr. Duffy. Mrs. Sinico's daughter testifies "her mother had been in the habit of going out at night to buy spirits" (111). Apparently she was sufficiently dispirited by the withdrawal of Mr. Duffy. The whole is a painful case, and the news article within the story is a brilliant fragmentary exposition of it.

"Grace" is the first story in which Joyce consciously tried for parodic reasons to structure his narrative on the basis of a pre-existing epic structure, in this case the three-part division of Dante's *Commedia*. Mr. Kernan suffers his epic descent or inferno on the pub floor, undergoes his cleansing in the purgatorial hospital, and finds paradisiacal grace in the Gardner Street church. It was Joyce's brother, Stanislaus, who knew from a conversation with Joyce that Dante's *Commedia* served to scaffold the story. "It is a simple pattern not new and not requiring any great hermeneutical acumen to discover – inferno, purgatorio, paradiso. Mr. Kernan's fall down the steps of the lavatory is his descent into hell, the sickroom is purgatory, and the Church in which he and his friends listen to the sermon is paradise at last."[10] Hell for this Dubliner is biting off part of his tongue in a drunken tumble down a flight of barroom stairs. Purgatory is to get off the sauce. Paradise is a Catholic service for commercial travelers. The joke, of course, was that the mock epic placed transcendent grace on the businessman's conversion experience, not all that far from the simony that rules the spiritual world of Dublin. After all, the last citation from the gospel in the story gets the text slightly wrong on purpose, substituting *die* for *fail* on the theory that Father Purdon does not want to see reprobates again after the secular grace he offers. As for what the text means, the priest is a good deal more certain than are those who stumble across it in Luke's gospel.

> For the children of this world are wiser in their generation than the children of light. Wherefore make unto yourselves friends out of the mammon of iniquity so that when you die they may receive you into everlasting dwellings. (173)

The dwellings are both gnomonic and ambiguous. At the end of "Grace" and with the version of grace that Joyce provides in *Dubliners*, readers all too often find themselves right back where they were when they began the volume, at the gates of hell.

4

Portrait of the Artist as a Young Man

"Voiceyversy"

Before he left for Europe in 1904 Joyce had an idea for a long auto-biographical essay on the childhood and education of a budding Irish artist, but the magazine *Dana*, run by several of his acquaintances in Dublin, passed on the opportunity. In a diary entry on his brother's birthday, February 2, 1904, Stanislaus Joyce sets out the sequence of the early work for *Portrait of the Artist as a Young Man*, emphasizing what is not usually thought its prevailing tone or mode of action.

> He has decided to turn his paper into a novel, and having come to that decision is just as glad, he says, that it was rejected. . . . Jim thinks that they rejected it because it is all about himself, though they professed great admiration for the style of the paper. . . . I suggested the title of the paper 'A Portrait of the Artist,' and this evening, sitting in the kitchen, Jim told me his idea for the novel. It is to be almost autobio-graphical, and naturally as it comes from Jim, satirical. He is putting a large number of his acquaintances into it, and those Jesuits whom he has known. I don't think they will like themselves in it. He has not decided on a title, and again I made most of the suggestions. Finally, a title of mine was accepted: 'Stephen Hero,' from Jim's own name in the book 'Stephen Dedalus.' The title, like the book, is satirical.[1]

The title Stanislaus suggested played on an adventure ballad called *Turpin Hero* and perhaps on the "moo-cow" myth at the beginning of the present *Portrait* in which children are spirited away by cattle, trained as heroes, and magically returned to their homes as gifted saviors for Ireland. Joyce wrote nine hundred manuscript pages, cast half of them into the fire, and did not live to see the remnant published as *Stephen Hero* in 1944. But he reprised the original title planned for the essay, salvaged some of the story line, and reconceived the effort, focusing on formational moments in a young writer's life.

Joyce begins *Portrait* with one of the most hackneyed narrative formulas imaginable – "Once upon a time" (3). The innovative artist ought to do better. And the artist soon does.

> Once upon a time and very good time it was there was a moocow coming down along the road and this moocow that was coming down along the road met a nicens little boy named baby tuckoo.[2] (3)

"Once upon a time" does not belong to the narrative so much as to the toddler's father who speaks it. He stares at his young child through the bottom of a glass so that the child imagines a kind of detached tale-talking face. Joyce understands the process at the beginning of *Portrait* when he parodies it in *Finnegans Wake*: "Once upon a drunk and a fairly good drunk it was and the rest of your blatherumskite!" (453). The effect of that first voice we hear in *Portrait* is crucial for the rest of the book, indeed for the rest of the young artist's career. Whose voice controls the "once upon a time"? And who speaks the blather, father or son?

At the conclusion of *Portrait* the writing voice changes to first person singular. Stephen appeals in his diary to his mythical father, the artist-artificer Daedalus, so that he might have the power to represent his real father representing him: "Old father, old artificer, stand me now and ever in good stead" (276). Joyce writes about the prospect of getting ready to write. No matter how much Stephen would wish to switch his name from Dedalus to Daedalus, he still speaks and writes the language of his father in Ireland. He even carries himself like his father. In *Ulysses* he remembers strolling down Parisian streets before he was called back to Dublin at the time of his mother's illness: "Proudly walking. Whom were you trying to walk like? Forget: a dispossessed" (3: 184–5).

In something like a mobius strip, *Portrait* works *ex post facto*.[3] Stephen emerges at the end to take back the voice that his father took from him at the beginning – "voiceyversy" (453) as Joyce describes it in *Finnegans Wake*. Better yet, Stephen supplements both his real father and the fathers of the Catholic Church who trained him in order to free himself from the constraints that then become the subject matter of Joyce's fiction. In the form Joyce presents the young artist, he is barraged by voices not his own. All his life "he had heard about him the constant voices of his father and of his masters" (88). "Yet another voice had bidden him to be true to his country" (88), and for Stephen "These voices had now come to be hollowsounding in his ears" (88). Even in *Ulysses* Stephen says he is weary of voices not his own: "I am tired of my voice, the voice of Esau" (9: 981). In *Portrait*, Stephen wrestles with the problem after one of his talks with the English Brother Michael.

> —The language in which we are speaking is his before it is mine. How different are the words *home, Christ, ale, master*, on his lips and on mine! I cannot speak or write these words without unrest of spirit. His language, so familiar and so foreign, will always be for me an acquired speech. I have not made or accepted its words. My voice holds them at bay. My soul frets in the shadow of his language. (205)

When Stephen as an adolescent visited Cork with his father he began to sense that a writer could take over memories not his own by conjuring from a "legend" carved in a desk:

> On the desk before him he read the word *Foetus* cut several times in the dark stained wood. The sudden legend startled his blood: he seemed to feel the absent students of the college about him and to shrink from their company. A vision of their life, which his father's words had been powerless to evoke, sprang up before him out of the word cut in the desk. A broadshouldered student with a moustache was cutting in the letters with a jackknife, seriously. Other students stood or sat near him laughing at his handiwork. One jogged his elbow. The big student turns on him, frowning. He was dressed in loose grey clothes and had tan boots. (95)

Stephen has not figured out whether he speaks or ventriloquizes, but he gets close here to a notion that Joyce develops through his career. There are those who are silenced by the voices around them, and there are those artists who have the power to call up the voices of others through their own.

"A Poor Trait of the Artless"

Portrait of the Artist as a Young Man borrows its title from writing's sister art, portraiture, and borrows its epigraph from Ovid's account in the *Metamorphoses* of the story of Daedalus, the Greek artist who fashioned wax wings to escape from the Cretan labyrinth. Any who know the myth know that there are two flyers at risk, Daedalus and his son Icarus. One soars in control of his resources; the other flies too close to the sun and melts his wings before he plunges into the Aegean. From what we see of Stephen in *Portrait* it is not certain which role he will play. The Daedalus–Icarus myth is poised between flight and crash. So is *Portrait*. Joyce had made the distinction clearly in *Stephen Hero* when he differentiated between classical (Daedalian) art as skilled, patient, contained, and satisfied, and Romantic (Icarian) art as overextended, hyperbolic, and bathetic.

> The romantic temper, so often and so grievously misinterpreted and not more by others than by its own, is an insecure, unsatisfied, and impatient temper which sees no fit abode here for its ideals and chooses therefore to behold them under insensible figures. As a result of this choice it comes to disregard certain limitations. Its figures are blown to wild adventures, lacking the gravity of solid bodies, and the mind that has conceived them ends by disowning them. (78)

The title Joyce chose at the behest of his brother is further bifurcated: artist/young man. Depending upon how one reads the title, the young man may not even be an artist or, at least, not one yet. The title could also mean what the artist looks like to a young man. Or what a mature artist sloughs off to become the artist he was not at the time of the portrait. In all cases – and I think all are possible – the question Joyce wants asked and answered is how well the young artist stares down the bovine monster, the Minotaur, in the labyrinth of his city?

> The letters of the name of Dublin lay heavily upon his mind, pushing one another surlily hither and thither with slow boorish insistence. His soul was fattening and congealing into a gross grease, plunging ever deeper in its dull fear into a sombre threatening dusk, while the body that was his stood, listless and dishonoured, gazing out of dark-

ened eyes, helpless, perturbed and human for a bovine god to stare
upon. (119–20)

In *Finnegans Wake* Joyce calls *Portrait* "a poor trait of the artless"
(114). He spends a good deal of time making fun of his own enterprise in writing about a writer who has so little to show: "his back
life will not stand being written about in black and white" (169).
And perhaps the best way to see Joyce's *Portrait* is to see it as less
about the artist than about the artist's material in search of a writer,
a book about the impress of various phenomena, about developing
senses, about sensibility, about sexuality, religiosity, intellect, aesthetics, politics. *Portrait of the Artist* is a training manual of sorts. In
sequence, as the book develops, the training involves family, school,
early reading, contacts with friends, young girls, prostitutes, even
(vicariously) the Irish peasantry, priests, and educators. Dedalus trains
in rituals – religious, dramatic, and poetic. He theorizes on the nature of art, and in the final chapter he writes a poem that the book
workshops for the benefit of its readers.

Throughout, Stephen's training consists in adjusting language to
the level of his sensual impressions and emotions. At various times,
Joyce invokes the basic senses – sight, sound, smell, taste, touch – to
reinforce his book's training regimen. He once told his Swiss friend
Adolf Hoffmeister that to "create something in a segment of time one
must employ all the senses: if one is omitted or is described with the
help of the others, the result is labored and lacks the proportions of
reality" (*Portraits of the Artist in Exile*, p. 130). The influx of stimuli on
the first page of *Portrait* poses the problem of sensation and differentiation. How does anyone select, shape, and understand sensual
stimuli? Later in *Portrait* Stephen offers two definitions of art within
several paragraphs that help set out a process Joyce follows, at least
at the rudimentary level. The first is lapidary: "to try slowly and hum-
bly and constantly to express, to press out again, from the gross earth
or what it brings forth, from sound and shape and colour which are
the prison gates of our soul, an image of the beauty we have come to
understand – that is art" (224). The second is Aristotelian: "—Art,
said Stephen, is the human disposition of sensible or intelligible matter for an esthetic end" (224). At each stage in his development,
Stephen focuses on the power of sensate experience in relation to
verbal experience as the ground of artistic representation.

In rapid succession on the opening page we experience all the senses at the artist's disposal in a sequence set by Joyce. The child, "baby tuckoo," hears a story, sees a "hairy face," imagines the taste of "lemon platt," sings "his song," feels the bed "warm and then it gets cold," smells the oilsheet, and dances to the piano's notes, *"Tralala."* The array of senses returns to narrative prominence in different ways in each chapter. When Stephen gives in to the kiss of one of his Nighttown prostitutes as an adolescent, his discriminatory powers dissipate as he goes into a kind of shock and his senses become a primordial soup.

> He closed his eyes, surrendering himself to her, body and mind, conscious of nothing in the world but the dark pressure of her softly parting lips. They pressed upon his brain as upon his lips as though they were the vehicle of a vague speech; and between them he felt an unknown and timid pressure, darker than the swoon of sin, softer than sound or odour. (108)

In the justly famous hell-fire retreat of *Portrait*'s third chapter, Stephen gives over all time and space to another narrative, and, in the process, gives over the senses to another narrator. "Retreat" is one of those Joycean words that bear a religious meaning, "a withdrawal for a while from the care of our life, the cares of this workaday world, in order to examine the state of our conscience" (117) and a secular one, backing off one's position. Stephen retreats from the "workaday world" as the narrative of the retreat imposes upon all his senses – sight, smell, sound, taste, touch.

> Every sense of the flesh is tortured and every faculty of the soul therewith: the eyes with impenetrable utter darkness, the nose with noisome odours, the ears with yells and howls and execrations, the taste with foul matter, leprous corruption, nameless suffocating filth, the touch with redhot goads and spikes, with cruel tongues of flame. (131)

When Stephen in the next chapter readies himself for the vocation of priest, he literally begins by letting religion do what the story of the retreat did, take the world away from him: "The world for all its solid substance and complexity no longer existed for his soul save as a theorem of divine power and love" (162). Stephen deserts his body along the path to a priestly vocation: he "felt himself passing out of it as if his very body were being divested with ease of some outer skin or peel" (161). Each "of his senses was brought under a rigorous discipline" (162), and within a single page Joyce provides a litany of mortifications, making Stephen avoid "every encounter with the eyes of woman," making him exert "control over his voice," disallowing "repugnance to bad odors," eschewing "the savors of different foods" (163). The most important mortification is the one of greatest significance to Joyce as artist, the sense of touch – precisely because the word means so many things to a writer's body and soul.

> But it was to the mortification of touch that he brought the most assiduous ingenuity of inventiveness. He never consciously changed his position in bed, sat in the most uncomfortable positions, suffered patiently every itch and pain, kept away from the fire, remained on his knees all through the mass except at the gospels, left parts of his neck and face undried so that air might sting them and, whenever he was not saying his beads, carried his arms stiffly at his sides like a runner and never in his pockets or clasped behind him. (163)

When the senses are suppressed the artistic vocation goes up in thin air and the priestly one seems the only choice left for Stephen. What happens at this point in the narrative is very interesting. Stephen tries to listen seriously as a priest at Belvedere readies to make an offer. The priest mentions the gowns worn by Dominican priests, "*Les jupes*, they call them in Belgium" (167), and Stephen by association travels back to Dublin's Nighttown.

> The names of articles of dress worn by women or of certain soft and delicate stuffs used in their making brought always to his mind a delicate and sinful perfume. As a boy he had imagined the reins by which horses are driven as slender silken bands and it shocked him to feel at Stradbrook the greasy leather of harness. It had shocked him too when he had felt for the first time beneath his tremulous fingers the brittle texture of a woman's stocking for, retaining nothing of all he read save that which seemed to him an echo or prophecy of his own state, it was only amid softworded phrases or within rosesoft stuffs that he dared to conceive of the soul or body of a woman moving with tender life. (168)

Stephen is done for. The text takes a step away from the priesthood even before Stephen does, almost like Satan conceiving sin in

Paradise Lost before he actually sins. Stephen's senses return here. He literally gets a different vocational feel, and his priestly career evaporates in the excitement and realism of sensual memory. It takes Dedalus only a few more pages to fall Icarus-like from the vocation of priest and – with a modicum of hope and talent – fly Daedalus-like into the realm of art: "The snares of the world were its ways of sin. He would fall. He had not yet fallen but he would fall silently, in an instant" (175). Stephen uses the language of Milton's Satan here, but the artist is of the devil's sensate party and revels in it. The life of the priesthood would simply not work for Stephen: "The wisdom of the priest's appeal did not touch him to the quick" (175). It did not touch him to life, which is what *quick* means, surely not so much as the touch of a woman's stocking. In *Finnegans Wake*, Joyce jokes about underwear and the artistic vocation. He has his artist figure Shem place a personal ad in the paper.

> Jymes wishes to hear from wearers of abandoned female costumes, gratefully received, wadmel jumper, rather full pair of culottes and onthergarmenteries, to start city life together. Jymes is out of job, would sit and write. He has lately commited one of the then commandments but she will now assist. (181)

Portrait's Workshop

Each chapter in *Portrait* is a snare and an opportunity for Dedalus. *Portrait* employs words that will end up configured in Stephen's famous credo at the end of the book: "O life! I go to encounter for the millionth time the reality of experience and to forge in the smithy of my soul the uncreated conscience of my race" (275–6). Each important word is charged here, and has appeared in some form early in the narrative, as if the object of the artistic vocation Stephen seeks is to put together the famous sentence near the end of the book he is in. The word *forge* carries the artist's double program, to make something new and to create an image of something that already exists (a counterfeit).[4] Joyce does both with Ireland. It is testimony to Joyce's foresight in *Portrait* that by the time of *Finnegans Wake* the young hero-artist goes by the name of an actual counterfeiter, Shem the Penman. The idea of the artist as maker and imitator, creator and

forger, prophet and profiteer, gets cleverly picked up in Joyce's rep-
lication of the mission of Coleridge's Ancient Mariner: "He prophets
most who bilks the best" (305).

Stephen is not yet privy to Joyce's ironic take on his activities. He
spends the book building towards the vocabulary with which he
ends. When as a lad he dreams of Mercedes, the heroine of Dumas'
The Count of Monte Cristo, he "wanted to meet in the real world the
unsubstantial image which his soul so constantly beheld. He did not
know where to seek it or how: but a premonition which led him on
told him that this image would, without any overt act of his, encounter him" (67). In the hell-fire sermon it "was his own soul going forth to experience, unfolding itself sin by sin" (110). When he
considers the priestly vocation he does so as an artist might: "ac-
complishing the vague acts of the priesthood which pleased him by
reason of their semblance of reality and of their distance from it"
(171), or in "vague sacrificial or sacramental acts alone his will seemed
drawn to go forth to encounter reality" (172). When he first thinks
of the Greek Daedalus before his artistic epiphany on the strand in
Dollymount he considers his name prophetic, "a symbol of the artist
forging anew in his workshop out of the sluggish matter of the earth"
(183), and he, too, "would create proudly out of the freedom and
power of his soul" (184).

Joyce carefully accumulates the Daedalian vocabulary in *Portrait*,
though he leaves the artist in mid-flight and it is not altogether clear
how Stephen-Icarus plans to land. What is certain is that the more
mature Joyce rarely lets the imagination soar without mooring it to
real and secure territory. By the last chapter the young artist reaches
the point where he can gather enough material from life to compose a poem about his jealous infatuation for a young woman and
his rivalry with a young priest. But readers should be wary of resting here; there is, after all, the book the reader is reading, which is a
much better testament to the developing artistic consciousness represented within it than the villanelle.

The real workshop of *Portrait* is in the various kinds of activity
that surround Stephen as he talks. In the middle of one of his excurses
on aesthetic beauty, the text interrupts Stephen's train of thought:
"A long dray laden with old iron came round the corner of Sir Patrick
Dun's hospital covering the end of Stephen's speech with the harsh
roar of jangled and rattling metal" (226). Joyce constructs the scene

so that the sounds of Dublin drown out Stephen's aesthetic ruminations, which is as it should be if the artist is true to the scene represented. From its title to its themes, *Portrait* is juxtapositional. The sights and sounds of Dublin are themselves a running commentary on Stephen's progress as an artist. Joyce learned from a master of novelistic language, Gustave Flaubert, that the language characters speak not only delineates action but also often serves as implicit counterpoint within a scene. The famous case is when in *Madame Bovary* Rodolphe sweet-talks Emma in the empty mayoral office while beneath the window a livestock auction takes places in the town square. In *Portrait* one of Stephen's most inspired reveries about his career takes place as he walks near Bull Bridge.

> His heart trembled in an ecstasy of fear and his soul was in flight. His soul was soaring in an air beyond the world and the body he knew was purified in a breath and delivered of incertitude and made radiant and commingled with the element of the spirit. An ecstasy of flight made radiant his eyes and wild his breath and tremulous and wild and radiant his windswept limbs. (183)

Stephen thinks of himself as Daedalus here, but the text would have him as Icarus. Several young friends nearby, diving into the breakwaters of the Bay, hail him as he walks by.

> —One! Two! . . . Look out!
> —O, cripes, I'm drownded! (183)

In *Ulysses*, Stephen finally gets the joke himself. He thinks of how quickly he returned home from Paris after leaving at the end of *Portrait*: "Couldn't he fly a bit higher than that, eh?" (3: 64). When he speaks with the Dean of Studies at University College, Stephen tries to distinguish between the rarefied language of aesthetics and the language of the marketplace, and runs into the very problem that artists have to learn to represent juxtapositionally. The point Stephen would make becomes confused in the making. He puts forward to the Dean an example: the word *detain*.

> The use of the word in the marketplace is quite different. *I hope I am not detaining you.*

—Not in the least, said the dean politely.
—No, no, said Stephen, smiling, I mean . . . (203)

The Dean's misunderstanding invites the marketplace in with a vengeance, and the scene itself represents the manner in which Joyce, at the very time Stephen searches for an example, provides one.

The last chapter of *Portrait* presents Stephen in attendance at University College with all the active intrusions of Irish life and even world politics. He writes a poem. The reader sees Stephen experience, observe, select, and revise. There are two tracks for the production of the villanelle: one is technical and involves the choice of verse form, rhyme scheme, set allusions; the other is emotional and involves the triangular jealousy at the root of so many plots for Joyce. In this instance the poem would not exist were it not for the rivalry for the affections of Emma represented by her friendship with Father Moran, a rivalry made worse by the unintended irony (on the Father's part) of his remark: "The ladies are with us. The best helpers the language has" (239). The wrong language, of course. Stephen cottons neither to the priest nor to his Gaelic. Rather, he writes a revenge poem or a love poem. On the technical side, the poem is about control and constraint (the Daedalian enterprise). On the emotional side the poem is about desire and its discontents (the Icarian disaster).

Stephen's villanelle is originally connected to Davin's lurid and alluring story about the Irish peasant woman who dragged him into her cottage on his way home from a football match. After Davin tells his story, the flower woman on the street says to Stephen, "Don't forget your own girl, sir!" (198). Stephen surely does not, and Davin inadvertently provides the *mise en scène* for Stephen's poem: "—O, come now, he said. Is it on account of that certain young lady and Father Moran! But that's all in your own mind, Stevie. They were only talking and laughing" (219). For Stephen, that is enough, enough that they were only talking and laughing, and enough that it was only in his own mind.

While at work on the poem Stephen theorizes about art: "The esthetic emotion (I use the general term) is therefore static. The mind is arrested and raised above desire and loathing" (222). But the artistic process can never divorce itself from the loathing and desire that make it up. Joyce rests more easily with the idea that the role of the artist is to reform and refashion the riot of emotions into

intelligible and discernible images and actions. Stephen's poem trans-
forms loathing and desire, and much more. In the middle of all the
white noise that surrounds its action, the chapter records Stephen
beginning to draw from the totality of his experience – randomly in
some instances – in order to put his poem together.

The enterprise truly begins inside Stephen's head, with lines of
poetry already there: Shelley's *"Art thou pale for weariness"* (102), John
Henry (Cardinal) Newman's *"that pain and weariness yet hope of better
things"* (177), and Ben Jonson's *"I was not wearier where I lay"* (190).
Stephen's villanelle begins, *"Are you not weary of ardent ways"* (236),
and we can see why. As he wanders through and around Dublin
Stephen adds to his store of material and poetic impulses. He sees
the jumble of language on street signs and advertisements, thinking
of a chaos of syllables and "wayward rhythms" (193), which of course
he holds in abeyance for his poem until he needs them. Material for
the poet keeps entering his head before he has a poem in which to
deposit it. At the physics lecture the professor recites a little verse of
W. S. Gilbert's about *"elliptical billiard balls"* (207). When Stephen
thinks of putting a "ball of incense" in his villanelle to image the
Catholic mass, he reconsiders after remembering the absurdity of
"an ellipsoidal ball" (236–7) and the anatomical reference one of his
mates shouts at the physics lecture: "—What price ellipsoidal balls!
Chase me, ladies, I'm in the cavalry!" (208). Stephen makes a silent
emendation and we see only, *"The chalice flowing to the brim"* (243).

But the real engine of the poem becomes clear when Stephen
listens to his friend Davin's remark about Stephen having dropped
out of the Gaelic League language class because of his old flame and
a young priest. From this point Stephen cannot get E. C. and Father
Moran out of his head – even in the midst of his theorizing about
art: "—Let us take woman" (226), Stephen says in grappling with
the idea of beauty, and the imagination of taking her or leaving her
in his life is what he ends up writing about, all poetry having recourse in some way or another to what Stephen says the Italian
physiologist Luigi Galvani calls a syncope, "the enchantment of the
heart" (231). Thus the "enchanted days" of the villanelle.

The poem actually appears in the text at about the same time its
muse appears.[5] Lynch says to Stephen: "—Your beloved is here"
(234). Stephen wakes as if from a dip in inspirational waters or the
other kind of Icarian wet dream: "Towards dawn he awoke. O what

sweet music! His soul was all dewy wet" (235). It is as if he were annunciated, with the "seraphim themselves" breathing on him. And he delivers the poem in like fashion.

> A glow of desire kindled again his soul and fired and fulfilled all his body. Conscious of his desire she was waking from odorous sleep, the temptress of his villanelle. Her eyes, dark and with a look of languor, were opening to his eyes. Her nakedness yielded to him, radiant, warm, odorous and lavishlimbed, enfolded him like a shining cloud, enfolded him like water with a liquid life . . . (242)

Stephen's jealousy of Father Moran again surfaces after he begins to put the stanzas of the villanelle together. No surprise then that the penultimate stanza of the poem reads:

> *While sacrificing hands upraise*
> *The chalice flowing to the brim*
> *Tell no more of enchanted days*
> (243)

Even after the poem he cannot get Emma out of his mind. He senses that she must be walking home in Dublin and he conjures her "wild and languid smell: the tepid limbs over which his music had flowed desirously and the secret soft linen upon which her flesh distilled odour and a dew" (254). So many scenes from Joyce flood in upon this one – the first sight of Mangan's sister in "Araby," the harp sequence in "Two Gallants," the "distant music" moment of "The Dead," and, not least, the crucial memory of the touch of a woman's underclothes when Stephen was considering the vocation of the priesthood. The erotics of art will return in *Ulysses*, mostly centered on the splendor in the grass Molly Bloom and Leopold enjoyed when he proposed on Howth Head.

In *Portrait*, at the very least, the artist has to learn to take what is given him. There is an interesting exchange when Cranly sings *Rosie O'Grady* and asks Stephen if he considers that poetry. Stephen answers that "—I want to see Rosie first" (266), and Cranly says, hinting at either E. C. or the ladies of Nighttown, "—She's easy to find" (266). Stephen continues to think about E. C., haunt her even, as she appears in one or another location in Dublin. He records in his diary that when she "Asked me, was I writing poems? About whom? I asked her" (275). About whom else?

5

Exiles

Ibsen in Dublin

Joyce's only play, *Exiles*, is a bourgeois fable of artistic freedom and sexual liberation, with the complicating comic notion that neither art nor sex is as liberating as the artist and lover imagines them to be. The artist in the play is more family man than writer, and husband, father, ratepayer in the bargain. No matter how strenuously he denies it, the artist is also a jealous husband trapped in a triangle farce of his own making. The ghost of Henrik Ibsen walks the boards with Joyce in a Merrion suburb of Dublin sometime around 1912.

The Abbey Theatre rejected the play during the war when Joyce hoped to stage it in Ireland, and then Joyce unsuccessfully attempted to mount it with any theater company in Europe that would have it. He told his friend Frank Budgen that another cuckold play, *Le Cocu Magnifique*, took the wind out of his play's sails for a Parisian production. He marked the theme of jealousy as central to both plays: "The only difference is that in my play the people act with a certain reserve, whereas in *Le Cocu* the hero, to mention only one, acts like a madman" (*Making of Ulysses*, p. 315). When Joyce did arrange for its production in 1919, after the war in Munich, *Exiles* flopped following a disastrous evening. Later, in 1924, it had a semi-successful run of forty-one performances in New York.

The action of the play is simple. An artist, Richard Rowan, returns from Italy with his common-law wife and young son. He has written a famous, though largely unread, book. His friend, Robert, wishes to get him an important teaching chair at University College, with the ulterior goal of keeping him in Dublin so that he might initiate an affair with Richard's common-law wife, Bertha. The artist figure is in some kind of crisis for reasons not fully explained, though it seems to have to do with the sense of guilt he feels for the strain he has put on Bertha for leaving Ireland with him in the first place nine years before. Richard says to Robert of Bertha what Leopold Bloom in *Ulysses*, if he could frame it quite this way, might say to Blazes Boylan, if he could understand it that way, of Molly Bloom.

> I would not suffer her to give to another what was hers and not mine to give, because I accepted from her her loyalty and made her life poorer in love. That is my fear. That I stand between her and any moments of life that should be hers, between her and you, between her and anyone, between her and anything. I will not do it. I cannot and I will not. I dare not. (69)

Bertha is a native of Western Ireland who wants to recover the initial intensity of a relationship that enabled her to leave her home and settle in Europe with a man of Richard's abiding strangeness. She wants and needs a renewed sexual and emotional connection from her husband, but threatens (not very convincingly) to seek the same from someone else should Richard continue to withhold his conventional affections. Richard's best friend Robert wants Bertha, though his want is neither cerebral nor spiritual – he simply wants. Beatrice, Robert's ex-lover and Richard's epistolary muse, wants to admire and feel admired, but desire in her, if it ever existed at all, has atrophied to Protestantism and piano playing. Not one of the characters in the play understands either his or her situation fully or honestly, let alone that of others. The crisscrosses and misunderstandings make for some extraordinary action, though clearly not to the taste of all readers or theatergoers.

Richard encourages the possibility of adultery as a test of free will, deeper spiritual commitments, and love's renewal. That is, he tries to redirect the angst of sexual betrayal by recharging the sexual energy of his own marriage, while blaming himself for the diminution of that energy in the first place. At least that is the surface reason Richard offers. In point of fact, Richard is unclear why he allows the possibility of adultery to play through. As the action develops, all we see is a sequence of nightmarish plots framed against the artist's unconventional behavior, most of them framed by the artist himself. Though Richard tries to convince himself he can articulate his states of mind and his reasons for testing conventional standards of fidelity within a relationship, his jealousy, paralysis, paranoia, and other insecurities are thoroughly indistinguishable.

The similarity to the plot of *Ulysses*, on which Joyce was working hard when he paused to write *Exiles*, surely cannot escape an alert reader. In a sense, *Exiles* is *Ulysses* under psychoanalysis. Ezra Pound called it "a necessary katharsis."[1] The play offers a sequence of glosses on the day of *Ulysses*, and even, retrospectively, on the evening of the long short story, "The Dead." Moreover, the best glosses on *Exiles* are actually provided by Joyce in a sequence of very full notes for the play, currently appended to the printed edition. What the play and its notes reveal is the centrality of the mediated love relation, in which jealousy is at once manufactured and eroticized. Joyce is deeply influenced here – and admits it in the notes – by the marriage scenarios worked out with almost exquisite pornographic energy by Leopold von Sacher Masoch in *Venus in Furs*: "The play, a rough and tumble between the Marquis de Sade and Freiherr v. Sacher Masoch" (124).[2] Simply put, sexual stimulation comes from the real or imagined adulterous liaisons a husband creates for his wife. Joyce is aware that he has refined the cuckold triangle farce into a much more complex play about fidelity and conscience. He writes in the notes to the play that in the cuckold plot "the centre of sympathy appears to have been esthetically shifted from the lover or fancyman to the husband or cuckold" (115). Sympathy provides "a technical shield for the protection of a delicate, strange, and highly sensitive conscience" (116). Joyce then writes an extraordinary note for the play that perversely applies to him, to Richard, and to Bloom in *Ulysses*, though Joyce was clearly playing to the masochist (literally the Leopold von Sacher Masoch) in him.

> Richard, unfitted for adulterous intercourse with the wives of his friends because it would involve a great deal of pretence on his part rather than because he is convinced of any dishonourableness in it wishes, it seems, to feel the thrill of adultery vicariously and to possess a bound woman Bertha through the organ of his friend. (125)

Joyce identifies the kernel of the action as Richard's "baffled lust converted into an erotic stimulus" (114). To effect that conversion requires "the very immolation of the pleasure of possession on the altar of love" (114). It is not difficult to imagine how such a prospect would turn the narrative theme of the faithful Penelope on its head in the *Odyssey*. When Joyce replaces the fidelity plot of the Homeric poem with the adultery plot of *Ulysses*, readers might well turn back to the parameters of the play *Exiles*, at least to see what Joyce thinks he is doing. If jealousy is to become erotic then fidelity cannot literally be an unadulterated prize.

The Dramatic Angle

Exiles may be a stilted piece of dramatic writing, a kind of cryogenic Oscar Wilde, but adultery plots always draw viewers and voyeurs in. The eternal question of "will she or won't she?" is always intriguing. Moreover, Joyce renders the question more ambiguously: "did she or didn't she?" He adds in a note to the play: "The doubt which clouds the end of the play must be conveyed to the audience not only through Richard's questions to both but also from the dialogue between Robert and Bertha" (125). Joyce described *Exiles* as "three cat and mouse acts" (123). The play sets out its design by putting its four main characters in varying sequences of triangular relations. The child, Archie, plays a minor but positioning role in the action. That the adult male and female characters are paired with the same first initial assists in the play's geometrical disposition.

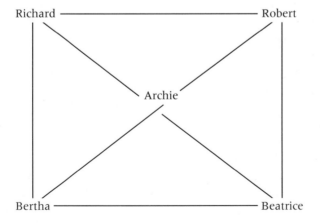

To change the figure at the point of mediation in every triangle is to see all the potential relationships in the play. There are four triangles, with each adult character mediating three. Archie innocently resides at the center of these figurations, almost as a silent nexus of future consequences. In one version of the action Robert and Richard are in rivalry over Bertha. In another version, Bertha and Robert are rivals for Richard. In a third, Richard is in rivalry with Bertha for Robert. In a fourth Bertha and Beatrice are rivals for Richard. Depending upon how one aligns the characters and reads the triangles, there can be as many as twelve plots with shifting points of mediation among the four main characters. If one counts all the possible triangles and the variety of mediators in which Archie appears, that adds four more – plus two more if one adds the names along the bisecting axis lines. This sounds absurd, but it is fine as far as Joyce is concerned – he sees drama as essentially a skeleton of the laws of human action. He wrote in his essay "Drama and Life": "Drama has to do with the underlying laws first, in all their nakedness and divine severity, and only secondarily with the motley agents who bear them out" (*CW*, 40).

The issues devolving from the play's geometry are ones that mark comic action. At the center is a sexually mordant common-law marriage. There is a deep love between Richard and Bertha, but an absence of satisfactory "touch." More comic action emerges from all this than one might expect, certainly if we judge from the clumsy conventionality of Robert Hand, whose emblem in the play is an overblown bunch of roses he brings Bertha. His name suggests his motive – he wants to get his hands on Bertha. To do so, he has to land Richard a job teaching comparative literature at Dublin's University College. But to manage that he has first to legitimize the artist newly returned to Catholic Ireland with an unsanctified wife and, nominally, a bastard child. Robert has to float a rumor that Richard and Bertha are actually married. That way he can draw the two of them back to Dublin sanitized and legalized in order to put himself in a position to follow the inclinations of his heart and cuckold his friend.

Richard is well onto this scheme, but instead of trying to stop it he tries to accelerate it. He knows the key ingredients of the scheme before it takes place. One cannot keep secrets from an artist: "I know everything. I have known for some time" (59). He has been tipped off by Bertha, so the cuckold plot plays side by side with a kind of author's farce. A note to *Exiles* touches on one aspect of Joyce's thinking, an almost willed sexual betrayal, at once feared and necessary: "Richard having first understood the nature of innocence when it had been lost by him fears to believe that Bertha, to understand the chastity of her nature, must first lose it in adultery" (119). "Chastity of her nature" is one of those Joycean phrases that seems religious but really translates into a secular version of free choice. Richard wants the sexual issue drawn to a crisis because for him love is not about bodily possession, though – as in most comedy – when it looks as if his wife will actually make love to his friend, Richard is racked by the very bodily jealousy he descried. He shows up at the point of assignation between his wife and Robert, and Bertha says to him: "You see, after all you are like all other men. You had to come. You are jealous like the others" (72). Bertha may be right, but that in itself would not be enough to stop Richard's plotting.

What does Richard really think he wants? He seems to want all in all. He wants artistic freedom, free love, married love, fame, worship. He wants loyalty commensurate with his own sense of specialness. He questions Robert on whether Robert has what it takes to take what he, Robert, wants.

> RICHARD: Have you . . . ? *He stops for an instance.* Have you the luminous certitude that yours is the brain in contact with which she must think and understand and that yours is the body in contact with which her body must feel? Have you this certitude in yourself?
> ROBERT: Have you?
> RICHARD, *moved*: Once I had it, Robert: a certitude as luminous as that of my own existence – or an illusion as luminous. (63)

Richard is a writer, though it is never made clear exactly what his writing is like, and he wants veneration not so much for his mind or his body but for the gift he has given Ireland by virtue of his work – a reputation clearly not measured in book sales. Nor is that veneration measured by the slight he perceives in one phrase buried in the article Robert writes about him in the newspaper: "Not the least vital of the problems which confront our country is the problem of her attitude towards those of her children who, having left her in her hour of need, have been called back to her now on the eve of her long awaited victory" (99).[3] The "hour of need" sends Richard over the deep edge. What he does not want is to be discomfited by any of the things he wants, nor does he particularly care what anyone else wants or needs. Richard Rowan in this respect is like other of Joyce's neurotic characters, James Duffy of the short story "A Painful Case," and Stephen Dedalus everywhere he appears in Joyce's fiction. Richard has no conventional responses he will admit to, though he lives in a conventional world. Joyce writes of Richard in his notes: "his character must seem a little unloving" (120). Bertha asks him one of the more unintentionally funny questions of the play – "Tell me, Dick, does all this disturb you?" (48) – and one is at a loss to know why it would or would not.

Richard seems to Bertha more and more unfaithful in his own particularly exhausting way. She resents that Beatrice thinks her happy: "Happy! When I do not understand anything that he writes, when I cannot help him in any way, when I don't even understand half of what he says to me sometimes!" (98). Bertha takes the conventional way out in assuming that Richard allows her license with Robert so that he can take up with Beatrice, "have complete liberty with – that girl" (53). Nothing is further from Richard's mind: he desires Beatrice as dyspeptic muse at the very most. There is an indication that Bertha understands the adultery scenario the way Molly does with Blazes Boylan in *Ulysses*; that is, that Bloom needs her to commit adultery as a cover to his own dalliances because he would never engage in them otherwise. Both women get their men wrong. Such a prospect seems unlikely for either Richard or Bloom. They prefer sex in the head, or in writing, or at a distance. For Richard, especially, it is not as if he feels any great need to connect himself sexually with many women. Rather, he feels the need to be able to say he has that right whether or not he particularly chooses to exercise it. It is part of the artist's liberty, which has a more psychic than actual manifestation.

At the end of *Exiles* we are left with the victory of hope over whatever constitutes experience. As much as Joyce tests the limits of social subject matter, he still falls back on the more stable idea that the mystical bond between a man and a woman transcends the sexual bond. By the end of *Exiles*, no matter what has occurred sexually, the lover, Robert, not the husband, Richard, is an emotional heap –

a loser, a renegade, abandoning the scene of the crime or violation. Bertha says what Bloom would no doubt want Molly to say, though Molly would be much less direct about it: "I want my lover. To meet him, to go to him, to give myself to him. You, Dick. O, my strange wild lover, come back to me again!" (112). There is another suggestive parallel between *Exiles* and *Ulysses*: "Sure he thinks the sun shines out of your face, ma'am" (90), Brigid the servant says to Bertha towards the end of the play, and Joyce echoes the line near the end of Molly's nighttime monologue in *Ulysses* when she remembers Bloom saying: "the sun shines for you today yes" (18: 1578). But in neither work is it clear what such sincere utterances mean for the future. Joyce prefers possibilities to resolutions.

6

Levels of Narration

"Preparatory to Anything Else"

The novelist Djuna Barnes met with Joyce socially at the café Deux Magots in 1922, the year of the publication of *Ulysses*, and recorded the occasion in a profile for *Vanity Fair*. Joyce said of all the controversy surrounding the publication of his book, "The pity is the public will demand and find a moral in my book – or worse, they may take it in some more serious way, and on the honor of a gentleman, there is not one single serious line in it." By serious Joyce meant metaphysical, transcendent, moralistic, preachy. He did not mean the book lacked the energy of life, the stuff of a real day, the hopes, fears, insecurities, pleasures, and absurdities of human life.

What questions are worth asking of *Ulysses*, "Preparatory to anything else" (*U*, 16: 1)? Joyce's enormous one-day encyclopedic account of eighteen hours of Dublin life on June 16, 1904 touches on an array of human emotions and experiences. The book is legitimately about isolation, pain, insecurity, laughter, love, memory, song, disappointment, and satisfaction. But readers should recognize that they have, in fact, dropped in for one day. It turns out to be an eventful day for each of the main characters, but neither they nor Joyce's readers have any way to measure even the next projected fictional day with complete confidence.

What readers can do effectively is track Joyce's sentences and discern the logic of the book's narration. There is no single inscribing principle that makes the whole of *Ulysses* comprehensible at once, but there are several smaller principles of narration that build towards a practical understanding of the day. Joyce ran a theater company, the English Players, in Zurich during World War I, and one of the roles he took upon himself for the company of mostly Irish and English rag-tag amateurs he collected for the troupe was official stage prompter. One member, an eighteen-year-old musician, Otto Luening, recalls Joyce shouting so loud from the prompter's box that the audience could hear him ten rows back.[1] *Prompter* may be one of the best ways to imagine Joyce's role as narrator of *Ulysses* as well.[2]

There are four distinct ways of conveying narrative information in *Ulysses*. Each has its own provenance and covers its own ground. I will list them below in the order in which they appear in the first chapter.

Third-person narration

Joyce begins with a very traditional mode of narration in which a neutral third-person voice describes what a reader needs to know in order to keep track of a scene, characters, time, locale, names, gestures, and of objects. The prose of third-person narration describes the rudiments of the day in *Ulysses*. It appears predominantly in the earlier chapters as the prevailing omniscient background voice, but third-person narration never disappears entirely from the text. The first paragraph of the opening chapter, "Telemachus," fits the bill precisely.

> Stately, plump Buck Mulligan came from the stairhead, bearing a bowl of lather on which a mirror and a razor lay crossed. A yellow dressinggown, ungirdled, was sustained gently behind him on the mild morning air. (1: 1–4)

There is not an incomprehensible word here, and for the most part all the skilled and graceful narration in *Ulysses* that makes up Joyce's third-person voice is crystal clear. The reader of course can bring powers of interpretation to bear on third-person narration, but what a reader chooses to do will not compromise a literal, plausible, comprehensible line sustained by that narration. The phrase "Stately, plump" may suggest to a reader the status of *Ulysses* as mock epic, or the crossed mirror and razor may carry whatever symbolic import the reader draws from it. But the actual narrative tells us what is not in dispute nor even in need of interpretation: a stately plump figure emerges from the stairhead of the Martello tower wearing a dressing gown and carrying shaving implements.

The goal of third-person narration is to set up the scene so that a reader can grasp what occurs and get a sufficiently detailed mental picture to satisfy what is a very basic narrative need. Third-person omniscient narration also reports on sounds and actions and events heard, seen, or felt by others. On the first page of *Ulysses* the narration tells us that Mulligan "peered sideways up and gave a long slow whistle of call" (1: 24). The text itself at this point does nothing to represent the whistle beyond reporting it.

For the most part, the third-person narration merely sets the scene, though sometimes it describes from an outside perspective a person's thoughts and feelings. In such instances the narrator knows what is inside another's head but the voicing is not coming directly from that person; instead we get the conventional "he thought" or "he felt" or "he fretted." A poignant example occurs early in *Ulysses* when a third-person voice approximates what a character thinks but records the pattern of thoughts in a perfectly conventional way. Stephen stands at the top of the Martello tower near Dublin Bay and thinks of his mother, recently dead and for whom he still wears mourning.

> Stephen, an elbow rested on the jagged granite, leaned his palm against his brow and gazed at the fraying edge of his shiny black coatsleeve. Pain, that was not yet the pain of love, fretted his heart. Silently, in a dream she had come to him after her death, her wasted body within its loose brown graveclothes giving off an odour of wax and rosewood, her breath, that had bent upon him, mute, reproachful, a faint odour of wetted ashes. Across the threadbare cuffedge he saw the sea hailed as a great sweet mother by the wellfed voice beside him. The ring of bay and skyline held a dull green mass of liquid. A bowl of white china had stood beside her deathbed holding the green sluggish bile which she had torn up from her rotting liver by fits of loud groaning vomiting. (l: 100–10)

The writing may be powerful, but Joyce penetrates into Stephen's mind as a knowing presence from outside that mind, recording the impressions and images belonging to Stephen's sensibility. We hear indirectly what a character sees, feels, remembers, thinks. In short enough order Joyce will find a different way to do the same thing – and much else – in *Ulysses*.

Sounded narration

Material in *Ulysses* that is sounded or spoken out loud is signaled, at least up until the "Oxen of the Sun" chapter, by a very clear device in the text: the printer's 2/em dash (—). Joyce uses the 2/em dash instead of quotation marks, which he felt marred the page. When a reader sees that dash the simple assumption is that something makes a sound that could be heard if one happened to be standing nearby. Mostly, the dashes enclose dialogue. If a character includes in speech the report of another's conversation or if a character reads aloud, Joyce will usually italicize that part of the sounded material still keyed by the 2/em dash. The reader of *Ulysses* reacts to spoken material much as one would in the midst of any scene from daily life. Some things spoken and heard are clearly registered and understood; others are not. But repeats, elaborations, rephrasings are in order and often requested by listeners. Few people speak in conversation with the goal of obscurity, and when they are obscure other characters react accordingly. Late in *Ulysses* Stephen says to Leopold Bloom about a knife on the counter of a cabmen's shelter at which Leopold Bloom partakes of coffee and a bun, "—Liquids I can eat, Stephen said. But O, oblige me by taking away that knife. I can't look at the point of it. It reminds me of Roman history" (16: 815–16). Nothing here is unheard by Bloom. He picks up the knife and thinks there is "nothing particularly Roman or antique about it" (16: 818–19). Bloom may not have caught Stephen's drift exactly, but the narration itself tells us precisely what Dedalus said, indicated by the 2/em dash, and we can take it from there, perhaps with better results than a weary Bloom.

The principle of sounded narration holds up in *Ulysses* until Joyce begins experimenting with other ways of presenting speech in later chapters, and readers who have gotten this far will have accumulated enough resources to deal with those experiments. Early on there are only a few exceptions to the rule of 2/em dashes and sounded speech. Joyce on occasion will have his characters imagine conversations that might take place. He will use the dashes inside a character's thoughts to represent those imagined conversations, as he does early in *Ulysses* when Stephen walks along the beach at Sandymount Strand and considers a visit to his aunt's house nearby: "Am I going to aunt Sara's or not?" (3: 61). Joyce records the conversation Stephen imagines with a 2/em dash: "—It's Stephen, sir" (3: 72). But Stephen fails to detour to his aunt's so we conclude no conversation took place: "Am I not going there? Seems not" (3: 158–9).

Interior narration

Interior narration is the record of unspoken, unarticulated material that circulates as either thoughts or silent dialogue inside a character's head. *Finnegans Wake* plays out interior narration as a kind of brain radio: "I have something inside of me talking to myself" (522). The principle is the same in *Ulysses*. If one were to have access to the thoughts of a reasonably intelligent or reasonably talented or reasonably aware person for one day, one would make certain assumptions. Those upon whose thoughts we eavesdrop would have a past history and would imagine, or at least expect, things from the future; they would mentally articulate some memories and hold others in reserve; they would have a store of knowledge on which they could draw; they would have manifest and marginalized hopes. Moreover, those unaware that another was privy to their internal thoughts would feel no need to explain them. A person walking down the street neither explains, nor in many instances even knows, why a sequence of thoughts enters the brain the way it does.

All of this seems plausible enough. Our own thoughts during the course of a day are often fragmentary, associative, bizarre, self-censored, and incoherent. We have wishes and desires that we sometimes sound out in silent phrases, and just as often do not. Our thoughts can be random, obsessive, repressed, indifferent, unsequential. So are those of Joyce's characters, and without the need for any excuses to us, his readers. To be true to the model Joyce sets up for interior narration requires that he not clarify internal thoughts for external consumption, as might a third-person narrator. The fiction of a reader bearing assisted witness to a character's thought is precisely what interior narration disavows. Witness is direct.

Unlike sounded narration in *Ulysses*, Joyce does not mark interior narration by any extraordinary punctuation. Those coming to *Ulysses* fresh often experience their first reading difficulty when interior thoughts flow directly out of third-person narration. But there are ways to mark those flow points. For one thing, interior thoughts tend to change narrative voice to first person and verb tense to present. Thinking occurs from a subjective perspective and in real time. If indicators of first person and present tense do not appear in interior thought, then there is another way to recognize its incursion. Idiosyncratic phrases or expressions mark interior as opposed to third-person narration. The first clear instance in *Ulysses* occurs on the first page in the midst of the description, just cited, of Mulligan's whistling teeth.

> He peered sideways up and gave a long slow whistle of call, then paused awhile in rapt attention, his even white teeth glistening here and there with gold points. Chrysostomos. Two strong shrill whistles answered through the calm. (1: 25–7)

The description begins in third-person narration past tense, but, obviously, the insertion of "Chrysostomos" jolts the passage out of its neutral stance. The reader pauses here, and not just to look up a name, but to wonder who speaks it or who thinks it. Maybe Mulligan? But there is no 2/em dash setting it off. It is not spoken aloud. Mulligan might be thinking it as an interior thought, and that would be plausible until the reader learns by experience that Joyce, at least until the tenth episode of *Ulysses*, enters no one's head but Stephen's or Leopold Bloom's. So the best guess is that 'Chrysostomos' signals a Stephen Dedalus thought entering the sentence, if ever so briefly. He sees Mulligan's open mouth and recalls a Greek orator whose name means golden-mouthed. The reader might know this, though it is far from likely. That Stephen makes a mental connection based on Mulligan's talking mouth and his capped teeth is all that matters because that is all that matters to him. Interior narration does not stop to tell us who Chrysostomos is. If it did, it would not be interior. More important, the reader knows that third-person narration ceases at this precise idiosyncratic moment because no neutral narrator would have any reason for popping such an unexplained name into a descriptive passage.

The first page of *Ulysses* provides the first word of interior narration proper, but the first time the reader encounters an extended

interior sequence of thoughts occurs just after Mulligan makes fun
of Dedalus' appearance and hands him a shaving mirror for a look.

> Stephen bent forward and peered at the mirror held out to him, cleft by
> a crooked crack. Hair on end. As he and others see me. Who chose this
> face for me? This dogsbody to rid of vermin. It asks me too. (1: 135–7)

The passage begins in the third person, but there is no way to
process "Hair on end" in the third person – the phrase belongs to
Stephen's thoughts. He frames the thought as he sees himself in the
mirror. And if he moves his lips silently when thinking "Who chose
this face for me?" then perhaps he sees the image in the mirror
asking him the question he has just posed, "It asks me too." In any
case, the third-person narrator has absconded the scene.

The next instance of interior narration reveals in fuller detail its
mechanisms. Buck Mulligan speaks to Stephen, using his nickname,
Kinch, and the narrative quickly moves into Stephen's interior
thoughts.

> —It's not fair to tease you like that, Kinch, is it? he said kindly, God
> knows you have more spirit than any of them.
>   Parried again. He fears the lancet of my art as I fear that of his. The
> cold steel pen. (1: 150–4)

At "Parried again" the narrative voice changes to interior. The verb
stays in the past tense because the action refers to past confronta-
tions, but the thought belongs inside Stephen's head. His next
thought shifts to present tense first-person. The passage is clearly
internal because if Stephen were speaking to Mulligan he would
not address him as "he." In the next moment, Mulligan, still speaking within the dialogue format, tells Stephen the two of them should
do something for Ireland.

> —God, Kinch, if you and I could only work together we might do
> something for the island. Hellenise it.
>   Cranly's arm. His arm. (1: 157–8)

Now the reader has a bit of work to do. Who is Cranly? There is no
2/em dash, hence Stephen thinks the phrase rather than speaks it.
Cranly is a name from Stephen's past. Those who recall *Portrait of the*

Artist may remember Cranly as Stephen's friend who made just the hint of a homosexual pass during a conversation at the end of the book. When Stephen hears Mulligan's "Hellenise it"[3] we can assume he thinks of Greek love, not Greek art. So the association with the homosexual Cranly makes perfect sense to Stephen, though the reader may be completely in the dark. That Joyce feels free to use an incident from an earlier book as a gloss on a later one is at once compelling and annoying, depending on how much a reader remembers or cares to. Joyce will do something like this many times in *Ulysses*, and that is why it is good practice to come to Joyce's later texts with an adequate sense of his earlier ones.

Soon enough Joyce takes matters even further. At Mulligan's mention of Kempthorpe, Stephen recalls something Mulligan must have told him about an incident never before narrated in this or any of Joyce's books, though it sounds as if the real-life Mulligan, Oliver St. John Gogarty, may have told the story. It is about a debagging incident that took place at Oxford when Mulligan studied there. Joyce's readers have just met Mulligan, so no one really has an advantage here by drawing from another Joyce text. We simply have to assume Stephen calls up a scene told him about a place to which he has never been.

> Young shouts of moneyed voices in Clive Kempthorpe's rooms. Palefaces: they hold their ribs with laughter, one clasping another. O, I shall expire! Break the news to her gently, Aubrey! I shall die! With slit ribbons of his shirt whipping the air he hops and hobbles round the table, with trousers down at heels, chased by the Ades of Magdalen with the tailor's shears. (1: 165–70)

To step back for a moment from all this is to see how Joyce will push at the barriers of interior narration. He is at once telling the reader that Stephen's train of thoughts are drawn from a deep reserve, something he has previously heard, and also that an artist, even a proto-one such as Dedalus, works by converting memory into narrative. Stephen's interior thoughts here recreate the scene. Even if the reader has little knowledge of the origin of the names and details, it is possible to imagine the process Stephen engages. He will need its resources again if he is to write narrative with any kind of a bite to it.[4]

Another feature of interior narration draws from material that the reader accrues along with the characters in *Ulysses*. When Stephen leaves the Martello tower early in the morning he goes to a day school in Dalkey run by a Mr. Deasy and teaches a short day before classes let out after ten. In the midst of a history lesson, a young student confuses the Greek general Pyrrhus with a pier.

> —A pier, sir, Armstrong said. A thing out in the water. A kind of bridge. Kingstown pier, sir.
> Some laughed again: mirthless but with meaning. Two in the back bench whispered. Yes. They knew: had never learned nor ever been innocent. All. (2: 32–6)

Stephen's interior narration obviously takes up at "Yes," but what is it the children know? A reader can guess that the pier is a meeting spot for lovers, but could do better by recalling exactly what Stephen recalls, a remark spoken two pages earlier by Haines, the English fellow staying in the Martello tower with Stephen and Mulligan, about their friend Seymour and a Carlisle girl, Lily: "—Spooning with him last night on the pier" (1: 700). Stephen would probably know that the pier was a spooning spot whether he had heard Haines say so or not, but the scrap of conversation helps the reader grasp how material builds up in *Ulysses*. Phrases and information from one chapter contribute to the thoughts that go through a character's mind in subsequent chapters, something that occurs all day long for both Stephen and Leopold Bloom.

Fourth-estate narration

Joyce has always been seen as making his greatest innovations in interior narration, but that is only half the story. Another kind of narration, one that is militantly exterior, manifests in *Ulysses* in ways rarely undertaken before Joyce in the history of novel form. It is almost as if another layer of narration runs parallel to the ones that advance the action, a narrative mode that is more supplemental than sequential. A good way to think of Joyce's supplementing material in *Ulysses* is to parallel it to the term for the press, the Fourth Estate, an addendum to the other three estates in France before the Revolution. Fourth-estate narration for Joyce is a kind of amalgam of commenting voices, that is, all the ways Joyce makes his presence felt in the text beyond the narrative levels designed to advance the specific actions and thoughts of his characters during the day.

The choice Joyce makes to overlap the events of the day of *Ulysses*, June 16, 1904, with the action of the Homeric *Odyssey* is the most prominent feature of fourth-estate narration throughout the book for the simple reason that the Homeric material is pure commentary: Joyce's characters have no idea that their lives are shaped by a plot over three thousand years old. Mulligan's spoken phrase, "Hellenise it" (1: 158) has no meaning for him in terms of what Joyce does in *Ulysses*, but every meaning for the reader trying to track Homer in the details of Joyce's narrative. The Homeric analogues all day long draw from casual remarks and descriptive observations that make supplemental sense for the reader only after they serve a perfectly plausible role in the course of action set out for the characters during the day. The one word of interior narration ending the first chapter of the book, "Usurper" (1: 744), is a natural thought for Stephen in the context of Buck Mulligan taking up psychic and physical space at the Martello tower. Moreover, Stephen himself has been thinking about Shakespeare's Prince Hamlet in the chapter so it is not inconceivable that the word 'usurper' enters his head in conjunction with Mulligan as a kind of Claudius, whose very nature is illegitimate. But "Usurper" also sets the fourth-estate parallel to the *Odyssey* in motion, a narrative that begins with a vacated kingdom, a missing father, and a bereft son, and a narrative that generates energy when Telemachus bitterly assesses the necessity of taking action against those who have dwindled his estate.

The first tangible appearance of visibly supplemental text in *Ulysses*, text that actually appears in the book as an incursion from beyond the narrative world so far, occurs with a series of press headlines inserted between paragraphs in the "Aeolus" chapter in news offices of the *Freeman's Journal*. It is as if Joyce announces the appearance of fourth-estate narration in *Ulysses* by actually inviting the Fourth Estate in. A headline places the chapter "IN THE HEART OF THE HIBERNIAN METROPOLIS" (7: 1–2); another names its characters, "GENTLEMEN OF THE PRESS" (7: 20); another waxes poetic on Ireland, "ERIN, GREEN GEM OF THE SILVER SEA" (7: 236). If a reader wonders about the supplementary status of those headlines, an easy experiment presents itself – take them out.[5] The main body of the text is completely unaffected and oblivious to the inserts.

"Extra!" is what newsboys used to shout on the street to sell papers, and *extra* is what most fourth-estate narration in *Ulysses* turns out to be. Much of the encyclopedic fullness of *Ulysses* derives from fourth-estate narration. Those moments in the book of sheer imaginative power – the Homeric parallels, the evolution of writing styles, the taxonomy of the chapters as parts of the human body (organ by organ), the Rabelaisian parodies of popular culture, the raw inclusion of information that a city catalogues as part of its ethos and history – all make up fourth-estate narration. Bloom gets in a row at Barney Kiernan's pub over the confusion surrounding a tip on a horse race, and the text takes off, launching Bloom from a Dublin neighborhood to the very reaches of heaven's gates. The parody of Revelations that ensues is extra text, value-added material.

> And the last we saw was the bloody car rounding the corner and old sheepsface on it gesticulating and the bloody mongrel after it with his lugs back for all he was bloody well worth to tear him limb from limb. Hundred to five! Jesus, he took the value of it out of him, I promise you.
>
>   When, lo, there came about them all a great brightness and they beheld the chariot wherein He stood ascend to heaven. And they beheld Him in the chariot, clothed upon in the glory of the brightness, having raiment as of the sun, fair as the moon and terrible that for awe they durst not look upon Him. And there came a voice out of heaven, calling: *Elijah! Elijah!* And he answered with a main cry: *Abba! Adonai!* And they beheld Him even Him, ben Bloom Elijah, amid clouds of angels ascend to the glory of the brightness at an angle of fortyfive degrees over Donohoe's in Little Green street like a shot off a shovel. (12: 1906–18)

If it seems to the reader that Joyce adds more and more supplemental material as the book progresses, the reader is right.[6] As the day advances the narration has more to remember about itself, almost a rolling stone that *does* gather more moss as it progresses over terrain. The book grows by remembering all that happens and reproducing versions of those events and circumstances in different narrative styles and formats. The headline inserts of "Aeolus" are the first example but from that point on Joyce adds supplemental material to the normal course of narration, from the Elizabethan language of the Shakespeare chapter, "Scylla and Charybdis" – "He came a step a sinkapace forward on neatsleather creaking and a step backward a sinkapace on the solemn floor" (9: 5–6) – to the prose fugue of "Sirens," the magazine-talk of "Nausicaa," the burlesques of "Cyclops," the gestating prose styles of "Oxen of the Sun," the wild visions of "Circe," and the depositions of "Ithaca."

One interesting exercise for readers at this point is to divide *Ulysses* into two virtual or conceptual columns, the first composed of all that happens in the text still based on the first three modes of narration – third-person, spoken dialogue, and interior narration – and the second composed of all that text printed in the book of which the characters have nothing to do first-hand. What a reader would discover is that the four longest chapters of the book – "Cyclops," "Oxen of the Sun," "Circe," and "Ithaca" – contain far and away the most supplemental narrative. Joyce has on the face of it separated characters out from the prose that surrounds them. The characters are not there working any more; or, if they are, they are transformed and rendered to the reader as something obviously different from who and what they were. Even the internal thoughts of characters late in the day appear to readers in a style commensurate neither with Bloom's nor with Stephen's way of expressing himself that we have garnered from earlier chapters, but in a way commensurate with the particular thematic subject of the chapter at hand. By the time of "Circe" and "Ithaca" the text even independently produces thoughts and speeches that recapitulate in sometimes accusatory and sometimes mocking form things that the book earlier represented as casual, random thoughts.

Fourth-estate supplements become almost the *raison d'être* of the "Circe" episode, in which the characters do relatively little while the book remembers everything it has placed in their minds and makes a hallucinatory spectacle of all that has been previously thought and acted. There are decidedly two tracks of action in "Circe," and unless readers have attained some aptitude at separating out the strands of narrative voicing they will be inclined to think that both Stephen and Bloom have a lot more to do with this chapter than they actually do. In effect, the book hallucinates alongside of them based on material it has learned from them. Playing on the sudden transformations of the magical "Circe" episode in the *Odyssey*, Joyce turns the action inside out, turns private public. What Joyce does in this chapter is allow his text the full expansive range of a world beyond social likelihood, beyond the constraints of law or physiology, beyond rational increments of time. There is no stopping the writer when he can disembody all the formulations of memory and desire, all the scenes and circumstances of social tribulation, all philosophical and spiritual systems, and anatomize them as textual supplements.

Mixed Modes

The difficulty for Joyce readers is that the four modes of narration in *Ulysses* are not always easy to separate. In the "Nestor" chapter Stephen glances at his student's copybook filled with arithmetic problems.

> Across the page the symbols moved in grave morrice, in the mummery of their letters, wearing quaint caps of squares and cubes. Give hands, traverse, bow to partner: so: imps of fancy of the Moors. (2: 155–7)

Where exactly here does interior narration begin? The passage clearly begins in third-person neutral narration. But does Stephen's interior thought pick up in the second clause or at the sentence break? Either is plausible, though most likely the third-person narrative describes what Stephen sees as he looks at the page of numbers just as traditional narrative would do, reporting from outside in. Stephen's thoughts take over at "Give hands." Here the idiosyncrasy of a command, issued as an interior thought, seems commensurate with the way Stephen frames his notions. Another instance that might cause some puzzlement occurs later in the "Nestor" episode when Stephen hears the action outside while speaking inside with Mr. Deasy, who alludes to God's ways.

> —That is God.
>   Hooray! Ay! Whrrwhee!
> —What? Mr Deasy asked.
> —A shout in the street, Stephen answered, shrugging his shoulders.
>   (2: 383–6)

A reader might wonder about the status of "Hooray! Ay! Whrrwhee!" There is no 2/em dash preceding it, as in the other lines of the passage, so at least by the standards of sounded action the shouts are not actually voiced. So what status do these words hold? Perhaps Stephen mimics in his mind the sounds he has heard a moment before. That is part of what goes on in his head all day long, a conversion of the Dublin material around him into forms suitable for narration, should he ever manage the task in print. Had Joyce chosen to put 2/em dashes around the same phrase, he would have done for *Ulysses* what Stephen practices in silence – write sounds. And that is why Mr. Deasy hears nothing. His "—What?" responds out loud only to Stephen's spoken "—That is God."

Another scene at the school encourages the reader to track the variety of ways Joyce mixes narrative levels. Before Stephen leaves his job for the day – indeed, for good it turns out – he promises to help the headmaster get a letter published in the local papers about the foot and mouth disease then raging in Ireland. Mr. Deasy has the sheet of his letter in the drum of his typewriter and pounds out the last sentences. The text signals what Deasy says out loud to Stephen by the appropriate reflex, the 2/em dash, but distinguishes between his words to Stephen and his reading aloud the sentence he types by italicizing the typing.

—Sit down. Excuse me, he said over his shoulder, *the dictates of common sense*. Just a moment. (2: 294–5)

Stephen stands by dutifully and then takes the letter Deasy hands him. The text then goes interior as Stephen glances over the sheet. Instead of Mr. Deasy sounding his typed sentences, Stephen's eyes silently take in phrases. Stephen does not read aloud – there is no dash as spoken marker – and the narration is not omniscient – it does not describe the sentences of the letter; rather, it posits a mind perusing things and reading quickly, including the fussy prose mannerisms of a schoolteacher.

May I trespass on your valuable space. That doctrine *laissez faire* which so often in our history. Our cattle trade. The way of all our old industries. Liverpool ring which jockeyed the Galway harbour scheme. European conflagration. Grain supplies through the narrow waters of the channel. The pluterperfect imperturbability of the department of agriculture. Pardoned a classical allusion. Cassandra. By a woman who was no better than she should be. To come to the point at issue. (2: 324–30)

The four levels of narration in *Ulysses* can work compactly in a word, a sentence, or a scene. There is a moment in the "Lotuseaters" episode when an acquaintance of Bloom's, M'Coy, reports on the loss of a mutual friend, while at the same time Bloom tries to catch a glimpse of a lady's ankle as she steps up on a tram. M'Coy relays his own spoken dialogue with two friends (italicized), Bloom thinks along other lines entirely, a third-person narration fills in the gaps, and the fourth-estate narration parallels the scene to Odysseus just getting a glimpse of home before he veers off course early in the *Odyssey*.

—*What's wrong with him?* he said. *He's dead,* he said. And, faith, he filled up. *Is it Paddy Dignam?* I said. I couldn't believe it when I heard it. I was with him no later than Friday last or Thursday was it in the Arch. *Yes,* he said. *He's gone. He died on Monday, poor fellow.*
Watch! Watch! Silk flash rich stockings white. Watch!
A heavy tramcar honking its gong slewed inbetween.
Lost it. Curse your noisy pugnose. Feels locked out of it. Paradise and the peri.
Always happening like that. The very moment. Girl in Eustace street hallway Monday was it settling her garter. Her friend covering display of. *Esprit de corps.* Well, what are you gaping at?
—Yes, yes, Mr Bloom said after a dull sigh. Another gone.
—One of the best, M'Coy said.(5: 126–36)

"Another gone," says Bloom out loud in conversation, but "another gone" in his thoughts is the opportunity for a leg shot lost at the tram stop. For the fourth-estate narration, the sight of home for Odysseus is gone with the wind that blows him away from Ithaca towards Lotusland.

For readers ready to test the limits of Joyce's fourth-estate narration, there are moments that allow the characters themselves to take the process part of the way before the exigencies of the day cut them off. At one point in the "Sirens" episode, Bloom thinks of Shakespeare, "Quotations every day in the year. To be or not to be. Wisdom while you wait" (11: 905–6). The text then continues in what seem his interior thoughts: "In Gerard's rosery of Fetter lane he walks, greyedauburn. One life is all. One body. Do. But do" (11: 907–8). The problem here is that the passage simply does not sound like Bloom – it is far too literary. And rightly so. It is a piece of text that appeared two chapters earlier when Stephen imagined Shakespeare walking down an Elizabethan street.

> Do and do. Thing done. In a rosery of Fetter lane of Gerard, herbalist, he walks, greyedauburn. An azured harebell like her veins. Lids of Juno's eyes, violets. He walks. One life is all. One body. Do. But do. (9: 651–3)

For years readers thought it a remarkable coincidence that Stephen and Bloom shared exact thoughts on the same subject. Of course they do not. The fourth-estate narration hears Bloom about to provide his version of Shakespeare and remembers the last time Shakespeare appeared in the text. So the narration retrieves Stephen's passage. Stephen is nowhere near Bloom at the time, nor was Bloom near Stephen when Stephen first thought the phrase. Even if Bloom had been, he could not have heard a thought. In this instance, the fourth-estate narrator, having produced in the "Sirens" chapter a prose imitation of a musical fugue, raided a previous chapter for a phrase repeatable as a musical motif. Readers have to grasp that the characters have nothing to do with this bit of supplementary activity in *Ulysses*. That is precisely the point of fourth-estate narration even when it borrows its phrases from material already in the book in another form.

There are many similar instances, especially in the later chapters of *Ulysses* when the book builds on its own memory bank of phrases and information for the express purpose of adding to the day a kind of textual presentation that we as readers have not seen before. Here is another brief moment from the fugal "Sirens": "Bloom ate liv as said before" (11: 569). Well, yes – the text did say it before in traditional third-person narration, the neutrally narrated first lines on Mr. Bloom, who "ate with relish the inner organs of beasts and fowls. He liked thick giblet soup, nutty gizzards, a stuffed roast heart, liverslices fried with crustcrumbs, fried hencod's roes" (4: 1–3). The fourth-estate supplemental narration reduces the phrase to "ate liv" precisely because the third-person narration had said it fully before. It can now come back as a variation on a phrase for a musical episode.

One of the most curious passages in all of *Ulysses* occurs at the end of the "Nausicaa" episode when evening falls and fireworks go off on Sandymount strand. The narration proceeds in a third-person panorama that Joyce's readers really have not experienced since the closing paragraphs of "The Dead" in *Dubliners*.

> A last lonely candle wandered up the sky from Mirus bazaar in search of funds for Mercer's hospital and broke, drooping, and shed a cluster of violet but one white stars. They floated, fell: they faded. The shepherd's hour: the hour of folding: hour of tryst. From house to house, giving his everwelcome double knock, went the nine o'clock postman, the glowworm's lamp at his belt gleaming here and there through the laurel hedges. (13: 1166–72)

At the end of the interlude – and it is an interlude because *Ulysses* so far has offered nothing so seemingly neutral and wistful at the same time – the third-person voice breaks down.

> Far out over the sands the coming surf crept, grey. Howth settled for slumber, tired of long days, of yumyum rhododendrons (he was old) and felt gladly the night breeze lift, ruffle his fell of ferns. He lay but opened a red eye unsleeping, deep and slowly breathing, slumberous but awake. And far on Kish bank the anchored lightship twinkled, winked at Mr Bloom.(13: 1176–81)

"Yumyum?" Who says that? There is no character here to absorb it as interior narration. And why does the lightship wink? Perhaps because the passage does too. After all, it stole its locution, "yumyum," from Bloom. A few paragraphs before Bloom reflected on the day he proposed to Molly Bloom on Howth Hill in the context of this present day in his marriage when another, Blazes Boylan, occupies his bed and enjoys his wife's favors.

> All quiet on Howth now. The distant hills seem. Where we. The rhododendrons. I am a fool perhaps. He gets the plums, and I the plumstones. Where I come in. All that old hill has seen. Names change: that's all. Lovers: yum yum. (13: 1097–1100)

Some of the interpretive fourth-estate moments woven into other levels of narration in *Ulysses* reveal Joyce operating at his sneakiest. He could not, in his wildest imagination, have imagined all readers would meet his gambits with the same degree of tolerance he reserves for himself in offering all of them up. Stephen Dedalus notices a picture of a horse who won the Grand Prix de Paris race in 1866 on his employer's Garrett Deasy's office wall: "*prix de Paris. 1866*" (2: 302–3). A chapter later Stephen walks along the Sandymount strand near the water's edge and thinks "Old Father Ocean. *Prix de Paris*: beware of imitations" (3: 483). Stephen connects "Old Father Ocean" with the sea-god Proteus, but why does he remember the picture on Deasy's wall? And why does he add the common advertising tag—"beware of imitations?" Because Stephen somewhere in his readings must have come across the story told by Herodotus, Strabo, and others that another prize of Paris, Helen of Troy, was kidnapped and taken to Egypt by a King Proteus, who then produced a fake image of Helen – a kind of magical hologram – for Paris to take to Troy. So the entire Trojan War was fought over an imitation. Helen's Greek husband, Menelaus, must stop off in Egypt after the war to get the real Helen back. Stephen apparently knows all this and that is why he makes the connections he makes.

What he does not know is what the fourth-estate narration counts upon. Joyce names the very chapter in which Stephen follows the train of his thoughts on Helen and King Proteus "Proteus," a parallel episode to the one in the *Odyssey* where Telemachus visits Menelaus who tells him about his trip to Egypt and his encounter with the sea-god Proteus. More than that, Joyce has himself produced an imitation of the whole *Odyssey* – an eighteen-chapter hologram called *Ulysses* that taps into a Homeric epic in so many intricate and bedeviling ways. "Beware of imitations" indeed! Joyce even goes a step further. When Leopold Bloom recalls the same advertising tag phrase he does so in relation to the Plumtree's Potted Meat ad that has coursed through the book: "Beware of imitations" (17: 604). The fourth-estate narrator then names the imitators as if they were Penelope's suitors in the *Odyssey*: "Peatmot. Trumplee. Moutpat. Plamtroo" (17: 604–5).

So far I have tracked Joyce's fourth-estate narration mostly as an interpretive overlay to the other forms of narration present in *Ulysses* – to third-person, sounded, and interior narration. But, as was apparent with the news headlines in the "Aeolus" episode, fourth-estate narration also produces supplemental texts for the book, texts that are at once separable from the day and intrinsic only to its comic and mock-epic dimensions. Even in these instances, though, the narration counts on the rest of the day for inspiration. At one point Joyce includes a public execution in the "Cyclops" episode as it might appear in the society pages of a hoity-toity newspaper. He is off on a riff that has almost nothing to do with any of his main characters at this point, but he draws his material from the only source in which he seems to have confidence, *Ulysses* itself. In the previous chapter, "Sirens," the baritone Ben Dollard entertained those gathered around the bar of the Ormond grill with an old Irish political ballad, "The Croppy Boy," about betrayal and a public execution in the 1798 Rebellion. The song and the political contexts set Bloom off (literally it turns out) on Robert Emmett, another executed patriot whose last words form the cadenza in the chapter, Bloom's fart: 'Pprrpffrrppffff' (11: 1293). But if Joyce needs a public execution for a supplemental interlude in his next chapter, he knows where to find it. Joyce executes Robert Emmett again in "Cyclops," as the entire modern world looks on in the shape of a delegation invited as witnesses by the Vice Regent of Ireland.

> The delegation, present in full force, consisted of Commendatore Bacibaci Beniobenone (the semiparalysed *doyen* of the party who had to be assisted to his seat by the aid of a powerful steam crane), Monsieur Pierrepaul Petitépatant, the grandjoker Vladinmire Poket-hankertscheff, the Archjoker Leopold Rudolph von Schwanzenbad-Hodenthaler, Countess Martha Virága Kisászony Putrápesthi, Hiram Y. Bomboost, Count Athanatos Karmelopulos, Ali Baba Backsheesh Rahat Lokum Effendi, Señor Hidalgo Caballero Don Pecadillo y Palabras y Paternoster de la Malora de la Malaria, Hokopoko Har-akiri, Hi Hung Chang, Olaf Kobberkeddelsen, Mynheer Trik van Trumps, Pan Poleaxe Paddyrisky, Goosepond . . . (12: 555–65)

This and other interludes in *Ulysses* seem more like the Marx Brothers' *Duck Soup* than anything resembling the realism of the day's action. But following Joyce in all the narrative venues that he takes the reader is a great part of the pleasure and challenge of *Ulysses*. Understanding the nature of those venues is an important first step for any reader.

7

Homer in *Ulysses*

"How You Fell from Story to Story"

The question occurs to every reader of *Ulysses* before reading a word of it: why the Homeric title? Joyce's book bears a title that nominally has little to do with the day represented in it. Homer's hero is never directly mentioned, though Stephen Dedalus speaks of Shakespeare's Ulysses from *Troilus and Cressida* twice, the Citizen in "Cyclops" mentions a Ulysses Browne, an Irish general in Maria Theresa's Austrian army, and Molly Bloom vaguely recalls an American, Ulysses S. Grant, visiting Gibraltar. When asked about the provenance of Christianity in Ireland, Dedalus explains to Bloom in "Ithaca" that St. Patrick was the initiating culprit, "by Patrick son of Calpornus, son of Potitus, son of Odyssus" (17: 33). Genealogies can always get a writer back where he wants to be, even if accidentally.

One would hope that any answer to the Homeric question reaches beyond the mere pleasure gleaned from recognizing the thousands of analogues to the precursor epic in Joyce's narrative, though that pleasure is not unsubstantial. Readers all too ready to dismiss such shenanigans as mere modernist wizardry miss a more important point. Part of the task of a writer whose scope projects as far and wide as Joyce's is to reflect the transmigration of values from one age to another, one culture to another. Joyce sets out to "steal our historic presents from the past postprophetical" (*FW*, 11). His play on *presents* makes the past a kind of gift to a modern writer, almost as if Homer predicts him: "Yet is nobody present here which was not there before" (*FW*, 613). The title of Joyce's last encyclopedic comic narrative, *Finnegans Wake*, derives from an Irish-American ballad about a hod carrier named Finnegan who falls off a ladder and plunges past the stories of the building he was fabricating – "how you fell from story to story" (374). When Joyce describes Finnegan's fall he also describes his own use of material from classical to Judeo-Christian times: "I want you, witness of this epic struggle, as yours so mine, to reconstruct for us, as briefly as you can, inexactly the same as a mind's eye view, how these funeral games, which have been poring over us through homer's kerryer pidgeons, massacree-doed as the holiname rally round took place" (515).

Joyce first conjured the title "Ulysses" for a short story in *Dubliners*, even pondering the title *Ulysses in Dublin* for the whole of the volume. After writing the last story, "The Dead," he thought he might add one more in which a reinvigorating Samaritan makes an appearance on the scene. An incident on which Joyce planned to base his story occurred to him a few days after he began seeing Nora Barnacle in June of 1904 at a time when he was still given to drinking heavily, so much so that one evening he got in a row near St. Stephen's Green and was aided by a man named Alfred Hunter.[1] Hunter took Joyce home, tried to clean him up and talk him back into relative sobriety until he could navigate the streets again. Good will and recuperative powers drew Joyce to the Homeric analogue for the Hunter story, but when he began to add what was generally known around town about Hunter's Jewishness and the wayward instincts of his wife the story got too big for its *Dubliners* britches.

In a conversation with Georges Borach in Zurich during August of 1917 Joyce elaborated on the Ulysses theme.

The most beautiful, all-embracing theme is that of the *Odyssey*. It is greater, more human than that of *Hamlet, Don Quixote*, Dante, *Faust*. The rejuvenation of old Faust has an unpleasant effect upon me. Dante tires one quickly; it is as if one were to look at the sun. The most beautiful, most human traits are contained in the *Odyssey*. I was twelve years old when we dealt with the Trojan War at school; only the *Odyssey* stuck in my memory. I want to be candid: at twelve I liked the mysticism in Ulysses. When I was writing *Dubliners*, I first wished to choose the title *Ulysses in Dublin*, but gave up the idea. In Rome, when I had finished about half the *Portrait*, I realized that the *Odyssey* had to be the sequel, and I began to write *Ulysses*. (*Portraits of the Artist in Exile*, pp. 69–70)

By summer of 1918 Joyce was well into the longer middle chapters of the book when he met a sculptor in Zurich, Frank Budgen, who became one of his better friends. Budgen recalls the early days of their acquaintance: " 'I am now writing a book,' said Joyce,' based on the wanderings of Ulysses. *The Odyssey*, that is to say, serves me as a ground plan. Only my time is recent time and all my hero's wanderings take no more than eighteen hours'" (*Making of Ulysses*, p. 15).

Joyce asks Budgen if he knows of "any complete all-round character presented by any writer" (p. 15). Budgen mentions Christ, Faust, Hamlet, and Joyce rejects them all as insufficient.

> "Your complete man in literature is, I suppose, Ulysses?"
>
> "Yes," said Joyce. "No-age Faust isn't a man. But you mention Hamlet. Hamlet is a human being, but he is a son only. Ulysses is son to Laertes, but he is father to Telemachus, husband to Penelope, lover of Calypso, companion in arms of the Greek warriors around Troy and King of Ithaca." (*Making of Ulysses*, p. 16)

Budgen questions Joyce further on what he means by complete man, and Joyce responds: "I see him from all sides, and therefore he is all-round in the sense of your sculptor's figure. But he is a complete man as well – a good man. At any rate, that is what I intend that he shall be" (17). Joyce emphasizes the point in *Ulysses* when even one of the day's no-goods, Lenehan, senses the *polytropic* qualities of Bloom: "—He's a cultured allroundman, Bloom is" (10: 581).

When a writer chooses to connect the details of one day in the life of a middle-class advertising canvasser in 1904 Dublin with the craftiest and most complete hero conceived in the epic tradition there is a natural tendency for readers to perceive the book as schizophrenic. But for Joyce the matter is differently disposed. He is helpful in describing the superstructure of *Ulysses* when he sends to the first translators and critics writing on *Ulysses* a set of *schema* with hundreds of Homeric analogues and other information.[2] He describes his work in a letter written in 1920 to Carlo Linati, his potential Italian translator.

> It is an epic of two races (Israelite – Irish) and at the same time the cycle of the human body as well as a little story of a day (life). The character of Ulysses always fascinated me – even when a boy.

Imagine, fifteen years ago I started writing it as a short story for *Dubliners*! For seven years I have been working at this book – blast it! It is
also a sort of encyclopaedia. My intention is to transpose the myth
sub specie temporis nostri. Each adventure (that is, every hour, every
organ, every art being interconnected and interrelated in the structural scheme of the whole) should not only condition but even create
its own technique. (*Letters*, I: 146–7)

Joyce provides a clue to his procedure in adapting the plot of the
Odyssey for the day of *Ulysses* when Stephen offers an intriguing title
for his hastily put together fable in the "Aeolus" chapter, about the
two women who climb Nelson's Pillar and drop plum pits down on
the city below. He calls it "*A Pisgah Sight of Palestine* or *The Parable of
The Plums*" (7: 1057–8). Professor MacHugh in the chapter registers
the analogy because of an earlier recited speech comparing the Irish
to the biblical Jews of the Exodus: "Moses and the promised land.
We gave him that idea" (7: 1061–2). The title and application work
because, as Professor MacHugh notes, new circumstances can reform around old plot lines. Leopold Bloom seems to have come to
the same conclusion when he considers the smaller gestures of life
that keep happening over and over, "history repeating itself with a
difference" (16: 1525–6).

Joyce was firmly convinced that the *Odyssey* itself borrowed its
plot from Phoenician accounts of off-shore and island navigations
from Semitic maritime logs.[3] In *Finnegans Wake* he called the super-
imposition of a Greek epic on Phoenician geographical tales
"Phenician blends" (221), and saw no reason why he should not be
credited with continuing what Homer started by taking "Our
homerole poet to Ostelinda" (445). Homer is always in motion –
that is why he writes odysseys. Joyce takes the epic beyond the Pillars of Hercules and sails it to Ireland on his "iberborealic imagination" (*FW*, 487), Iberia to Hibernia.

The choice that Joyce makes in naming *Ulysses* after the Latin name
for Odysseus instead of the original Greek merely reinforces the choice
he makes in adapting the story in the first place. The Latin "Ulysses"
already moved the Greek story west in Virgil's *Aeneid*. Dante takes
Ulysses to the Pillars of Hercules at the western end of the Mediterranean and then dumps him over the edge of the world. Joyce resur-
rects the fallen hero and moves him further west, stopping along the
way to pick up Molly Bloom, whose birthplace is Gibraltar.[4]

The Artist's Odyssey

Among all Odysseus' talents displayed in the *Odyssey*, the one that fascinated the mature Joyce most was the hero's powers of narration. Odysseus, after all, narrates nine of the ten years of his story; he crafts the tale he is in. One of the characters in the Library chapter in *Ulysses* notes that Coleridge reserved the epithet 'myriadminded' (9: 768) for Shakespeare, a nice English equivalent of polytropic, which was the first epithet bestowed on Odysseus by Homer. Polytropic means well-versed. Joyce would like to think of himself in the same way, as an all-rounder and, ultimately, a returner. The arc of the Odyssean plot turns on Joyce's larger conception of a career of an exiled artist representing the best hope for his moribund land. As hero, the artist presents himself as an Irish redeemer. Perhaps that is why Joyce titled his first attempt at autobiographical narrative *Stephen Hero*.

"ITHACANS VOW PEN IS CHAMP" (7: 1034) reads one of the mock headlines in the "Aeolus" chapter. Penelope wins the day and the hero in the *Odyssey*, and the "Penelope" chapter rounds out the day of *Ulysses*. But in the context that counts for Joyce the pen is champ, far mightier than the sword, and he headlines his case for writing as supremely heroic.[5] The sequences and struggles of Joyce's own writing career become part of the strata of the Homeric story: usurpation, exile, rivalry, silent and cunning strategic return. The true heroic action of his book, as he said on any number of occasions, is the writing of it, just as so much of the story inside *Finnegans Wake* concerns its production as a book – the setting of its type, the run of its pages on the printing press, the reading of its galleys, even the preparation for its critical reception.

The best allusions and parallels in *Ulysses* are those that get to the gist of what Homer's epic conveys for heroes, artists, and even ad men. Joyce builds the specific patterns of allusions to Homer's narrative at almost every instance, but he also builds a thematic ethos. If Joyce's mission is, in part, to revive an Irish presence in world literature, one that in the past spread "throughout the continent a culture and a vitalizing energy" ("Island of Saints and Sages," *CW*, 154), he has help from the words of Stephen Dedalus, who sets up the possibility of an epic connection when he points out that Ireland is a land of "All kings' sons. Paradise of pretenders then and now" (3: 316–17). If so, Ireland is a good place to remap an old epic. "Pretenders" is what Joyce's characters are as Homeric prototypes, but they are also epic claimants.

When Leopold Bloom at the burial site in the "Hades" chapter of *Ulysses* notes how those gone tend to be forgotten, "Out of sight, out of mind" (6: 872), he also sums up the *Odyssey* in relation to the missing hero. For those usurpers, demythifiers, and debunkers on the home island there is no prospect of return or homecoming, which for Joyce is the source for imaginative life. In the first episode, Haines' question to Stephen about belief gets to the heart of the matter. Nominally God is at issue, but the real question is about the essence of the plot of human renewal, a plot that controls the *Odyssey*, and that guides the day of Joyce's *Ulysses*: "Either you believe or you don't, isn't it" (1: 622–3). Either you believe it possible that June 16, 1904 can be a compacted parallel version of the ten-year *Odyssey* or you do not.

Joyce of course rearranges the *Odyssey* as much as he parallels it in *Ulysses*. Bloom has a daughter rather than a son,[6] and to the extent he serves Stephen as father, he does so at a symbolic remove. Bloom is not even sure he will ever see Stephen again, and the questioner of the "Ithaca" chapter asks why. Bloom answers in the catechistic form of the episode: "the irreparability of the past" (17: 975) and the "imprevidibility of the future" (17: 979). Stephen's search for a father in Bloom is by no means a done deal, nor is it certain from Stephen's perspective that such a search is even part of his consciousness: "Paternity is a legal fiction. Who is the father of any son that any son should love him or he any son?" (9: 844–5). Molly Bloom is hardly the faithful Penelope. Home rule is not secured in one day. Even the famous immovable bed of the *Odyssey*, the one built from the trunk of a rooted tree, has no certain provenance in Joyce's *Ulysses* – Bloom places its origins on Gibraltar; Molly notes "he thinks father bought it from Lord Napier" (18: 1213–14). But Molly fails to tell him that her father bought it from an old Jew named Cohen, and she fails to tell us whether Cohen lives in Dublin or Gibraltar. Much of the adaptation of the Odyssean plot takes place with full comprehension on Joyce's part that epic solutions for one day in the life of a novel are not only unavailable, but also unrealizable. The Blooms' marriage prospects are not once and forever resolved or ruined by whatever takes place during the day. We never know where Dedalus goes in the early hours of the next day after he leaves Bloom's apartment. Life holds as much likelihood of future crises as of acceptable resolutions.

Whatever the irresolute qualities of Joyce's Homeric adaptation, he works during the day to provide his readers with a sense of what is crucial for the action of both the *Odyssey* and *Ulysses*. "—Yes. Make room in the bed" (1: 713), Buck Mulligan shouts before he jumps in the sea at the forty-foot hole for a swim, and he echoes the goal of the suitors in regard to Penelope in the *Odyssey*, the threat of the living arrangements at the Martello tower for Stephen Dedalus, and the crisis in Bloom's and Molly's marriage. Those who take up space in the bed control the home front. That has not changed for three thousand years. Molly Bloom may not be Homer's version of the faithful Penelope, but she has a kind of fidelity to the reality of human circumstances around the world, and it is fitting that she has the last say on the application of Homeric material to the modern world and those who sail the sea in it: "the voyages those men have to make to the ends of the world and back its the least they might get a squeeze or two at a woman while they can going out to be drowned or blown up somewhere" (18: 853–5).

8

Three Dubliners

"Loveless, Landless, Wifeless"

Any reader approaching *Ulysses* and expecting a fully resolved plot or even full revelation of the primary characters' actions is going to be in for a big disappointment. One of the most sensible ways to approach *Ulysses* is to ask a more pointed question about each important character. What do Stephen, Bloom, and Molly lack and what do they want? These are generative questions because they get to the core of human matters in Joyce's work. Answers are not always easy to come by. What characters want or need is in some instances ambiguous and in other instances contradictory, but in all instances worth pursuing.

Early in *Ulysses*, Stephen recalls the wild goose or political exile, Kevin Egan, a revolutionary Irishman he visited in Paris: "Loveless, landless, wifeless" (3: 253). How close do the primary male characters of *Ulysses* come themselves to these conditions? Stephen bills himself as loveless – "Who will woo you?" (9: 938); he exiles himself from his abode at the Martello tower – "I will not sleep here tonight. Home also I cannot go" (1: 739–40); and a wife is out of the question – he can barely get over the elopement of his favorite prostitute, Georgina Johnson, with a traveling salesman. And how does Leopold Bloom fare? "Are you not happy in your home you poor little naughty boy?" (5: 246–7) asks Bloom's amatory correspondent Martha Clifford. Readers later learn the bare truth. The death of an infant son Rudy a few days after his birth altered the Blooms' sexual practices. Unlike many Irish households in a Catholic land,

Leopold and Molly Bloom, only children themselves, did not look upon infant mortality as a reason to stock the flat with replacement parts. It has been over ten years since the Blooms have enjoyed sex of the potentially procreative sort: "there remained a period of 10 years, 5 months and 18 days during which carnal intercourse had been incomplete, without ejaculation of semen within the natural female organ" (17: 2282–4).

As for landless, Joyce told his friend Jacques Mercanton that he made Bloom a Dublin Jew "because only a foreigner would do. The Jews were foreigners at that time in Dublin. There was no hostility toward them, but contempt, yes, the contempt people always show for the unknown" (*Portraits of the Artist in Exile*, p. 208). Bloom's outsider status is reinforced subtly all day long. Mr. Deasy in "Nestor" asks Stephen why Ireland is not plagued by the Jews of Europe, and answers: "—Because she never let them in" (2: 442). In one sense, *Ulysses* itself gives the lie to that notion, but in another Bloom remains outside even though he is a Jew Ireland let in. At Barney Kiernan's pub later in the day the locals are still on Bloom's case: "—What is your nation if I may ask?" (12: 1430). Though he converted once to Protestantism and twice to Catholicism, Bloom cannot cancel the Jewishness of his nature, nor does he particularly want to. The narrator in "Ithaca" questions

> —What, reduced to their simplest reciprocal form, were Bloom's thoughts about Stephen's thoughts about Bloom and about Stephen's thoughts about Bloom's thoughts about Stephen?
> He thought that he thought that he was a jew whereas he knew that he knew that he knew that he was not. (17: 527–31)

With a little care the reader can replace the pronouns with proper nouns: Bloom thought that Stephen thought that Bloom was a Jew whereas Stephen knew that Bloom knew that Stephen knew that Stephen was not. There is a divide inside Dublin and Bloom will always be on the side that most of the country's Catholic citizenry are not. Joyce wants readers to get this point because it controls the day. What everyone thinks is not always articulated, but it is always there. By working the pronouns of this small passage the reader comes directly up against one of the true barriers in *Ulysses* to Bloom's acceptance as a Dubliner.

When Bloom wonders why Molly, half a Jew herself and from Dublin via Gibraltar, picked him above others he recalls Molly's answer: "Why me? Because you were so foreign from the others" (13: 1209–10). In the heated prose parody of the "Oxen of the Sun" episode we hear of Bloom's Jewish, hence Eastern origins, though his family was Ashkenazi and from Hungary.

> The lewd suggestions of some faded beauty may console him for a consort neglected and debauched but this new exponent of morals and healer of ills is at his best an exotic tree which, when rooted in its native orient, throve and flourished and was abundant in balm, but, transplanted to a clime more temperate, its roots have lost their quondam vigour while the stuff that comes away from it is stagnant, acid, and inoperative. (14: 935–41)

The polemicist wonders: "Has he not nearer home a seedfield that lies fallow for the want of the ploughshare?" (14: 929–30). To what degree does this all add up to wifeless? Many Dubliners, not just the louts at Barney Kiernan's, have their doubts about the focus of Bloom's marriage. Lenehan gets a good laugh out of M'Coy when he reminds him of Bloom gazing at the stars in the jarvey while he fixed on Molly's breasts: "I was lost, so to speak, in the milky way" (10: 570). Given Molly Bloom's afternoon tryst with her singing tour manager, Blazes Boylan, the very least Bloom can expect is the epithet bestowed by the priest's clock in "Nausicaa."

> *Cuckoo*
> *Cuckoo*
> *Cuckoo*
> (13: 1289–91)

Stephen

As he was in *Portrait*, Stephen Dedalus is still very much a figure of in-betweenness. He is in between vocations, employments, lovers, countries, friends, acquaintances, even meals, and baths. He is controlled by paradoxical compulsions and obsessions: fear of water, fear of dogs, fear of thunder, the compulsion to disconnect from other beings, the obsession to remain untouched, insular, free. He

has desires and phobias, and an abiding sense of rivalry and paranoia. He lacks a supportive family, reliable confidants, an inspiring
female lover, and active prospects. On the day of the book, and by
his own set of directives, he quits his living quarters and his job.
What he clearly needs is a change, and he is much less sure than he
was at the end of *Portrait* what that change ought to be. Stephen
spends most of his day in *Ulysses* drinking and talking. The book
tracks him to at least three pubs, and during the hours missing from
that part of the day Joyce narrates we can assume he was imbibing
at others.

However desultory his day, though, Stephen has not yet given up
or given in. At one point he hears the whir of the dynamos from the
powerhouse and he imagines himself between the throbbing sounds
he hears in the air and the throbbing from his heart.

> I between them. Where? Between two roaring worlds where they
> swirl, I. Shatter them, one and both. But stun myself too in the blow.
> Shatter me you who can. Bawd and butcher were the words. I say!
> Not yet awhile. A look around. (10: 823–7)

At the same time that Joyce presents Stephen at loose ends in Dublin he wrote a poem about his own relations with the Irish Revival
movement, a matter that comes up with Dedalus in the Library chapter of *Ulysses* when he feels shunned by a group of local poets: "See
this. Remember" (9: 294). Joyce's poem "The Holy Office," set in print
at his own expense, pictures the 22-year-old Joyce as at the bottom
of the reject pile of the Revivalists, "the sewer of their clique."

> I, who dishevelled ways forsook
> To hold the poets' grammar-book,
> Bringing to tavern and to brothel
> The mind of witty Aristotle
> (*CW*, 149)

The young Joyce of "The Holy Office" is the one we see at the end of
Portrait and the beginning of *Ulysses*. The verses help explain some of
Stephen's civic and cultural paranoia.

> Where they have crouched and crawled and prayed
> I stand the self-doomed, unafraid,

> Unfellowed, friendless and alone,
> Indifferent as the herring-bone
> (*CW*, 152)

Bloom asks Stephen in "Eumaeus," "why did you leave your father's house?" (16: 252), and Stephen answers: "To seek misfortune" (16: 253). He has found it. Joyce sympathizes with Stephen to an extent, but also issues a warning that there is a limit to measuring anyone on potential alone, artist or citizen. Vincent Lynch reacts to Stephen's mock gesture in circling his hair with a coronal of vineleaves: "those leaves, Vincent said to him, will adorn you more fitly when something more, and greatly more, than a capful of light odes can call your genius father. All who wish you well hope this for you" (14: 1117–19).

At the end of *Portrait* Dedalus hoped that he had finally located his own voice amidst the din of those oppressing him in Dublin, but at the beginning of *Ulysses*, the first person who speaks is Buck Mulligan, conducting a mock Introit to the Catholic mass from the parapet walk of the Martello tower in the bay. The artist was the one who was supposed to take over the priest's role, and here that role is doubly usurped by the mocker. Dedalus seems paralyzed in the face of Mulligan's sheer expansiveness, and he has something else to worry about in the bargain. One undercurrent during the day of *Ulysses*, and presumably for a short time past – especially with the arrival of the Englishman Haines at the tower – is Stephen's fear that the home activities are not to his taste. Stephen thinks of his foot inside one of the shoes he has borrowed from Mulligan: "foot I dislove" (3: 448–9). Then by association he recalls the scene at the tower he inhabits.

> Wilde's love that dare not speak its name. His arm. Cranly's arm. He now will leave me. And the blame? As I am. As I am. All or not at all. (3: 451–2)

Stephen's "As I am" apparently does not include how they might like him to be, and his notion early in the book is that if one of the mates is going to leave the tower, it might just as well be him first. Stephen is fiercer on the subject when Mulligan in the Library chapter refers to "the charge of pederasty brought against the bard" (9: 732) and Stephen stares at his friend and thinks: "Catamite" (9: 734).

I am not sure that Stephen would disagree with James Duffy of the *Dubliners* story "A Painful Case": "Love between man and man is impossible because there must not be sexual intercourse and friendship between man and woman is impossible because there must be sexual intercourse" (108).

The sense of threat Stephen feels from the situation at the tower recesses to the background of the day's activities until Mulligan and Stephen are later involved in some sort of dispute at the Westland Row train station, not narrated in the book but alluded to by Bloom at the cabmen's shelter. Bloom seems to share in a general suspicion of Mulligan, and he adds the English chap, Haines, for good measure: "it was perfectly evident that the other two, Mulligan, that is, and that English tourist friend of his, who eventually euchred their third companion, were patently trying as if the whole bally station belonged to them to give Stephen the slip in the confusion, which they did" (16: 263–7).

In one of the finer ironies of the book, Stephen's concern about the advanced state of sexual aestheticism at the Martello tower does not help him deal with Bloom later that evening, partly because he has to get over a hurdle placed by the very Mulligan he distrusts. When at the door of the National Library that afternoon Mulligan and Stephen see Bloom passing through towards the portico, Mulligan says to Stephen

> —The Wandering jew, Buck Mulligan whispered with clown's awe. Did you see his eye? He looked upon you to lust after you. I fear thee, ancient mariner. O, Kinch, thou art in peril get thee a breechpad. (9: 1209–11)

The text is careful to point out that when Stephen and Bloom finally begin to talk at length late at night, their conversation turns to the "alternatingly stimulating and obtunding influence of heterosexual magnetism" (17: 25–6). Stephen has been nervous all day, and even though he is kinder and more open than he usually is with Bloom he still treats his stay at Bloom's flat gingerly by singing a song about Jewish ritual murder just to keep Bloom on the defensive. Bloom does not know quite what to make of the song, but neither does he know what Mulligan has said of him offhandedly earlier in the day. In the meanwhile, Stephen walks out into the early morning air never to be heard from again in Joyce's fiction, but perhaps to re-appear in printed form under another name, as Mulligan tells Haines he well might: "—Ten years, he said, chewing and laughing. He is going to write something in ten years" (10: 1089–90).

Bloom

Joyce told Ezra Pound that he had taken Stephen as far as he could take him this day, and that he was more interested in the deeper reserves of experience, toleration, and discretion possessed by Leopold Bloom. At a basic level, Bloom shares Joyce's abiding gen-tleness, his pacifism, his preference for the comic over the tragic, his veneration of love: "—Love, says Bloom. I mean the opposite of hatred" (12: 1485). One could mock the simplicity of Bloom's re-mark, as do the patriots at Barney Kiernan's pub, but sometimes for Joyce, and maybe sometimes for humanity, the simplest is the most serving. Joyce thought of Bloom as a good man, and throughout the day of *Ulysses* his only acts of meanness or mean-spiritedness are minor, as when he makes fun of the grammatical mistake in Martha Clifford's letter: "Wonder did she wrote it herself" (5: 268–9).

Bloom's life in Dublin is not a happy one. He has few close friends to speak of and only a few to speak to; he lacks a satisfying job and his marriage is in the midst of a dispiriting crisis. His only child has left home; he has lingering memories of his second child's early death at eleven days, and his father's sad suicide still haunts him. Though Bloom is a member of the Masonic League, he seems cut off even from practitioners of that curious craft. As we learn in "Ithaca," matters are getting worse the older he gets: "He reflected that the progressive extension of the field of individual development and experience was regressively accompanied by a restriction of the con-verse domain of interindividual relations" (17: 63–5).

At home, Bloom faces a different set of obstacles. The change in his and Molly's sexual life after the death of their infant son is a problem: "Could never like it again after Rudy. Can't bring back time. Like holding water in your hand" (8: 610–11). Molly and Bloom have not been talking in any depth about anything for the run of the past nine months since the onset of their daughter's menses: "a limitation of activity, mental and corporal, inasmuch as complete mental intercourse between himself and the listener had not taken place since the consummation of puberty, indicated by catamenic hemorrhage, of the female issue of narrator and listener, 15 September 1903" (17: 2284–8).

To grasp Bloom's situation on the day of *Ulysses* is to understand that he is threatened not just by the impending affair between Boylan and Molly that afternoon, but by habits building for years. In an extraordinary moment during the "Lestrygonian" episode Bloom ponders the increasingly love-starved condition of his life. He sits sadly at Davy Byrne's pub mid-day: "Stuck on the pane two flies buzzed, stuck" (8: 896). The image replicates his own marital state, and recalls him to a better time the day he proposed to Molly on Howth sixteen years before. This passage more than any suggests why Bloom must do all that he can to vitalize his marriage if he thinks there is even a spark of energy left in it.

> Wildly I lay on her, kissed her: eyes, her lips, her stretched neck beating, woman's breasts full in her blouse of nun's veiling, fat nipples upright. Hot I tongued her. She kissed me. I was kissed. All yielding she tossed my hair. Kissed, she kissed me.
> Me. And me now.
> Stuck, the flies buzzed. (8: 913–18)

What Bloom needs is reconnection to a living, breathing human being, primarily to his wife. There are repeated hints that Bloom wants another child or, at least, to think about that prospect, though perhaps *need* is too strong a word in this case. Like Stephen he is not ready to give up, and what he says after walking out of the cemetery grounds at Paddy Dignam's funeral holds for much of his life: "Plenty to see and hear and feel yet. Feel live warm beings near you. Let them sleep in their maggoty beds. They are not going to get me this innings. Warm beds: warm fullblooded life" (6: 1003–5). Bloom repeats the renewal motif at various times during the day, enough so that it serves his nature: "The new I want" (13: 1104).

Mostly it is a new Molly he wants, or a new Bloom in relation to Molly. He has to find a way of touching her. *Touch* is a word that appears often in Joyce. It is a word of tactile experience – touch of hands, lips, bodies, textures, sensations, inspiration, sexuality, humanity. Touch is the material power of representation: "a touch of the artist" (10: 582). It is the power of reproduction: "Give us a touch, Poldy. God, I'm dying for it. How life begins" (6: 80–1). It is excitation: "O wonder! Coolsoft with ointments her hand touched me" (8: 904–5). It is the start of a friendship: "the surety of touch" (17: 289). Those who do not touch – those who shy away, who hit, who refrain, who insulate – are those who are untouched in Joyce's world. For those who consider Joyce at best a cerebral, detached, hyperborean modernist, it pays to count the number of times those represented in his works are excited by touching, desire it, need it, feel they want it. Leopold Bloom will do everything in his power to touch Molly Bloom by the end of the day in *Ulysses*, and his desire is literal and metaphoric. He wants that more than anything, and some of the things he does to assure her being touched are things that might shock or surprise a conventional reader of bourgeois fiction.

Molly

On the day of *Ulysses*, Molly Bloom spends most of her time in bed, which makes one of her old standby songs, *Stabat Mater*, both a commentary and a critique. She lacks a manifest sense of her own worth, and it is difficult to tell whether confidence exists just below her surface or just above. In the short range – which on the book's terms means next week in her concert tour to Belfast – she seeks a venue to reassert herself in some viable way, musically and sexually. Molly Bloom needs a lover, and Blazes Boylan will do for the interim – "I got somebody to give me what I badly wanted" (18: 732–3) – but if he does not work and Bloom does not come back into the fold, then she says "Id like a new fellow every year" (18: 782): "what else were we given all those desires for Id like to know I cant help it if Im young still can I its a wonder Im not an old shrivelled hag before my time living with him so cold never embracing me except sometimes when hes asleep the wrong end of me" (18: 1397–1401). In essence, she needs to feel desired in a way different from the way Bloom desires her, or she needs at least to feel that Bloom is capable of desiring her in a way that brings her more comfort and more confidence than she currently possesses.

Ulysses does not assure any of its primary characters that they will fulfill all their needs satisfactorily in the course of this one day. But it does put Stephen, Bloom, and Molly in motion – with varying degrees of intent – in regard to what they lack and need even if they cannot altogether articulate these things to others or even to themselves. Stephen is much more unnerved than he lets on by the haze of homosexuality that hangs over the life of the Martello tower, and Bloom never reveals even in his thoughts the extent of the role he may have played in abetting Molly's liaison that afternoon with Blazes Boylan. Molly, for her part, remains undecided not only about what she plans for the future but what she plans for the next week.

Bloom spends part of his day trying to nail down the continued run of an advertisement on behalf of Alexander Keyes, tea merchant. He makes what arrangements he can to firm up commitment on both sides – merchant and newspaper – for the ad. The text names the client in one of its headlines in the "Aeolus" chapter: "HOUSE OF KEY(E)S" (7: 141). The headline emphasizes by parentheses two keywords of the book, with Molly's last word, "Yes" buried as one of the keys in "keyes." Neither Bloom nor Stephen holds in his possession the keys to the particular homes towards which each claims proprietary rights. Stephen has given his to Mulligan and Bloom has forgotten his in another pair of pants. The phrase that accompanies the ad – "Innuendo of home rule" (7: 150) – is the phrase that touches on the Odyssean quandary in the book. Does the son have rights in his father/mother land? Does the husband have the key to his own abode? Does Stephen give his key away for a reason? Does Bloom forget his accidentally on purpose? Home rule then becomes as much a challenge as an innuendo. At the end of the day, readers have no idea where Stephen plans to sleep and Bloom has not yet secured the Keyes ad, but as Stephen says in the Library chapter, "life is many days, day after day" (9: 1044).

9

Reflexive Fiction

"See This. Remember"

One of the more useful critical observations about *Ulysses* is that the book contains within itself the best clues on how to read it. Things that make perfect sense in the context of the narrative at hand will also make sense in the reading zone of *Ulysses*, that reflexive space where Joyce seems to reach out to his readers with help or in consolation.[1] After over six hundred pages of *Ulysses*, some of them at least not on the surface easy reading, Joyce has Molly Bloom comment offhandedly, "O Jamesy let me up out of this pooh" (18: 1128–9). Is she speaking on behalf of Joyce's exhausted readers? In similar fashion, when discussing the Latin of the mass text Bloom says, "More interesting if you understood what it was all about" (5: 423–4). Many react just that way to *Ulysses*. In the "Aeolus" chapter Stephen watches a newsman light a cigar:

> I have often thought since on looking back over that strange time that it was that small act, trivial in itself, that striking of that match, that determined the whole aftercourse of both our lives. (7: 763–5)

Stephen's tone is mock melodrama, but no one in the history of modern fiction has struck a better match than Joyce in superimposing the Homeric *Odyssey* over a Dublin day.

There are moments in *Ulysses* when the text paces out the action for readers, almost to let us know there is a consciousness behind the design of the book. Towards the end of the first chapter Buck

Mulligan is about to dive into Dublin Bay at the forty-foot hole near the Martello tower for a swim. He exchanges a few words with another swimmer who mentions a mutual friend in Westmeath: "—I got a card from Bannon. Says he found a sweet young thing down there. Photo girl he calls her" (1: 684–5). Mulligan replies, "—Snapshot, eh? Brief exposure" (1: 686). Two chapters later we learn that Leopold Bloom's daughter, Milly, had just taken a beginning position as a photographer's assistant. Bloom reads her letter – "I am getting on swimming in the photo business now" (4: 400–1) – which also mentions that a "young student comes here some evenings named Bannon" (4: 406–7). Mulligan's casual sexual quip, it turns out, was Joyce's way of providing Milly Bloom, a photo girl, her first brief exposure in *Ulysses* even before Joyce or the book names her.

Joyce always reviews the day for the reader in a way that either forecasts or recapitulates the action. Stephen sees Bloom following him in Dublin's Nighttown and thinks: "A time, times and half a time" (15: 2143). His language is that of the New Testament, but also recalls the times he has run into Bloom during the day: a time briefly at the National Library mid-day, a full chapter's time at the Lying-in Hospital on Holles Street at ten in the evening, and now "half a time" halfway through the Nighttown episode. Joyce offers more substantial reviews of the day of *Ulysses* when he supplements the text with material extrinsic to it. The Daughters of Erin recite a litany of prayers that essentially repeats the episodes of *Ulysses* chapter by chapter from the point of Bloom's entrance into the text, "Calypso," through to the present moment in the "Circe" chapter.

> Kidney of Bloom, pray for us
> Flower of the Bath, pray for us
> Mentor of Menton, pray for us
> Canvasser for the Freeman, pray for us
> Charitable Mason, pray for us
> Wandering Soap, pray for us
> Sweets of Sin, pray for us
> Music without Words, pray for us
> Reprover of the Citizen, pray for us
> Friend of all Frillies, pray for us
> Midwife Most Merciful, pray for us
> Potato Preservative against Plague and Pestilence, pray for us.
> (15: 1941–52)

The same kind of reflexive recapitulation of the day appears in "Ithaca" when Bloom's chapters comically transform into a series of Judeo-Christian ritual acts, reflecting Joyce's notion from the beginning of his career that any single action reflects a host of comparable adventures, activities, sequences, ceremonies.

> The preparation of breakfast (burnt offering): intestinal congestion and premeditative defecation (holy of holies): the bath (rite of John): the funeral (rite of Samuel): the advertisement of Alexander Keyes (Urim and Thummim): the unsubstantial lunch (rite of Melchisedek): the visit to the museum and national library (holy place): the bookhunt along Bedford row, Merchants' Arch, Wellington Quay (Simchath Torah): the music in the Ormond Hotel (Shira Shirim): the altercations with a truculent troglodyte in Bernard Kiernan's premises (holocaust): a blank period of time including a cardrive, a visit to a house of mourning, a leavetaking (wilderness): the eroticism produced by feminine exhibitionism (rite of Onan): the prolonged delivery of Mrs Mina Purefoy (heave offering): the visit to the disorderly house of Mrs Bella Cohen, 82 Tyrone street, lower, and subsequent brawl and chance medley in Beaver street (Armageddon): nocturnal perambulation to and from the cabman's shelter, Butt Bridge (atonement). (17: 2044–58)

Joyce reprises the chapters of *Ulysses* in *Finnegans Wake*, where he still busily recapitulates the action of his previous book's day with a Wakean list of Homeric episodes.

> Ukalepe. Loathers' leave. Had Days. Nemo in Patria. The Luncher Out. Skilly and Carubdish. A Wondering Wreck. From the Mermaids' Tavern. Bullyfamous. Naughtsycalves. Mother of Misery. Walpurgas Nackt. (229)

At times in *Ulysses* it seems as if Joyce has his readers directly in his sights. Two questions crop up in the first chapter about access to the Martello tower that serve those trying to gain access to the book. Mulligan asks, "Have you the key?" (1: 322), and "Did you bring the key?" (1: 532). In the National Library around two o'clock, Stephen prods himself and the reader with the same phrase: "See this. Remember" (9: 294). When Stephen seems to go off track in "Scylla and Charybdis," it is as if Joyce has a colloquy with his own audience: "What the hell are you driving at? I know. Shut up. Blast you.

I have reasons" (9: 846–7). The narrator in "Oxen of the Sun," in the style of John Ruskin, arrives on the scene with some good note-taking advice: "Mark this farther and remember" (14: 1379).

The first spoken words out of Leopold Bloom's mouth address a cat but also notice the book's reader: "O, there you are" (4: 17). Stephen kindly helps one of his lost students with a math problem in the "Nestor" episode and asks the question that Joyce might of those who are beginning to figure out his devices: "—Do you understand now? Can you work the second for yourself?" (2: 161). Something similar occurs when Stephen closes his eyes walking along the strand in "Proteus" and compliments himself: "I am getting on nicely in the dark" (3: 15). The dog roving the beach in the "Proteus" chapter is in much the same place as Joyce's readers scanning for Homeric references: "Looking for something lost in a past life" (3: 333).

On occasions the text of *Ulysses* provides readers with packaged commentary on the action. One of Bloom's thoughts in "Aeolus" tells us what to think about a spelling conundrum, "Silly, isn't it" (7: 169), while a headline in the same chapter tells us what we ought to think about a news story, "CLEVER, VERY" (7: 674). Skin-the-Goat's poker face in the "Eumaeus" episode strikes Bloom as amusing, and we concur: "Funny, very!" (16: 600). Bloom almost gets hit by a sand strewer in Nighttown, and remarks, "a chapter of accidents" (15: 2380), which is exactly what "Circe" is. "Ithaca" tells us that Bloom sought out Shakespeare "more than once for the solution of difficult problems in imaginary or real life" (17: 386–7), and that is just what happens in the Library chapter of *Ulysses* when Stephen does the same. Molly Bloom thinks, "if I only could remember the 1 half of the things and write a book out of it the works of Master Poldy yes" (18: 579–80), and Joyce comes as close as he can to doing just that.

Often material in the text serves as a reading prompt. When Stephen walks the strand at Sandymount he looks at the sea spawn and sea wrack and thinks, "Signatures of all things I am here to read" (3: 2). So are we. We read what Stephen reads and we read Stephen who is there for us to read him. Stephen tries to imagine the stuff strewn on the beach with his hands over his eyes as he walks and thinks what is in front of him and to the side, what he calls in German the "*Nacheinander*" (3: 13) – the after each other – and "*Nebeneinander*" (3: 15) – the next to each other. In a larger venue, these brief narrative phrases – things put in sequence and things juxtaposed side by side – explain the way Joyce sets the hour-by-hour events of a single day in Dublin against the actions in the Homeric *Odyssey*.

In the "Nestor" episode, one of Stephen's students appeals to the same impulse that governs Joyce's version of the narrative master plot: "—Tell us a story, sir. —O, do sir. A ghost story" (2: 54–5). Two hours later Stephen complies in the Library chapter when he tells a ghost story that reflexively serves Homer's Odysseus, Christ's martyrdom, King Hamlet's murder, Shakespeare's trek to London, the return of Parnell to Ireland, and Stephen's own trip to Paris and back.

> —What is a ghost? Stephen said with tingling energy. One who has faded into impalpability through death, through absence, through change of manners. Elizabethan London lay as far from Stratford as corrupt Paris lies from virgin Dublin. Who is the ghost from *limbo patrum* returning to the world that has forgotten him? (9: 147–51)

Stephen finds himself in "Circe" reformulating the collapsible plots of *Ulysses* while trying, as we have already seen in *Portrait of the Artist*, to speak aesthetics over the din of Dublin's street noise.

> What went forth to the ends of the world to traverse not itself, God, the sun, Shakespeare, a commercial traveller, having itself traversed in reality itself becomes that self. Wait a moment. Wait a second. Damn that fellow's noise in the street. Self which it itself was ineluctably preconditioned to become. *Ecco!* (15: 2117–21)

"*Ecco!*" or "there it is" finds its homology in English, echo, which is the way Joyce supposes all plots repeat in a different register, from solar myths to novels about the Dublin day of a commercial traveler. Even the day's advertisements, distributed all through the text of the book, replicate in miniature the action of the *Odyssey* reduced to the local paraphernalia of an urban metropolis.

> *What is home without*
> *Plumtree's Potted Meat?*
> *Incomplete.*
> *With it an abode of bliss.*
> (5: 144–7)

Bloom sees the ad early in the day, and then later notes that it is placed in the newspaper over the obituary columns, the right spot for its particular language, but also the right spot in a book modeled on the return of a hero who most everyone in the *Odyssey* thinks dead.

Wherever one turns in *Ulysses* Joyce is ready with material that casts light on the enterprise he engages. A tiny moth from "Circe" plays a reflexive role.

THE MOTH

I'm a tiny tiny thing
Ever flying in the spring
Round and round a ringaring.
Long ago I was a king
Now I do this kind of thing
On the wing, on the wing!
Bing!

(15: 2468–75)

Bloom helps explain how he, too, long ago – at least in Joyce's imagination – was a Homeric king, when he defines a word that Molly cannot understand from one of her romances, *Ruby: The Pride of the Ring*: "—Metempsychosis, he said, frowning. It's Greek: from the Greek. That means the transmigration of souls" (4: 341–2). As Bloom expands, he marks his own transmigration from Homeric to modern times.

> —Some people believe, he said, that we go on living in another body after death, that we lived before. They call it reincarnation. That we all lived before on the earth thousands of years ago or some other planet. They say we have forgotten it. Some say they remember their past lives. (4: 362–5)

Prompts exist in *Ulysses* for its writing as well as its reading. One of the headlines in the "Aeolus" episode reads: "HOW A GREAT DAILY ORGAN IS TURNED OUT" (7: 84). *Ulysses* itself is a daily organ, and, as Joyce said to his friend Frank Budgen, an epic of the human body. He puts the organs together chapter by chapter.[2] In the Library chapter Stephen tries to put together an account of Shakespeare that is at once theory and story, and instructs himself on what Joyce displays in *Ulysses*: "Local colour. Work in all you know. Make them accomplices" (9: 158). When he finishes Mr. Best says, "—I hope Mr Dedalus will work out his theory for the enlightenment of the public" (9: 438–9), and later, "You ought to make it a dialogue" (9: 1068–9). Joyce did both. Near the end of the chapter Mulligan supposedly quotes Yeats on Lady Gregory's Irish Revival works: "One thinks of Homer" (9: 1165). Well, that is precisely the point for Joyce, though not about Lady Gregory, rather about his *Ulysses*.

If *Ulysses* takes up its own writing as one of its themes, Joyce is on hand to sign on as author. Stephen notes that Shakespeare, like Michelangelo, finds a way of signing his name all over works: "He has hidden his own name, a fair name, William, in the plays, a super here, a clown there, as a painter of old Italy set his face in a dark corner of his canvas" (9: 921–3). We see the artist at work in *Ulysses* as well, partially in the guise of the ad man Bloom: "WE SEE THE CANVASSER AT WORK" (7: 120) reads a headline from "Aeolus." The only bit of script reproduced in the book, in the midst of so many words set in type, are the lyrics attached to the written bars of music for the "Little Harry Hughes" song in "Ithaca" (17: 801ff.). The handwriting is Joyce's, as even a non-expert can tell by just a simple comparison to a holograph page of the book's manuscript.[3] Joyce recorded only one passage aloud from *Ulysses*, the Tayler speech recited in "Aeolus" by a character named J. J. O'Molloy, whose name at least begins with Joyce's initials. O'Molloy signifies son of Molly, the product, in a way, of the book's muse. Joyce thus reads in his muse's voice.

Joyce works on many linguistic levels in *Ulysses*, and either his characters or his text often hit upon phrases that serve some of the reflexive themes of the book. Bloom notices that his daughter is a younger version of his wife, "Molly. Milly. Same thing watered down" (6: 87). The printed letter thinned down from an "o" is an "i." In "Circe" the text provides the diminution: "Milly, Marionette we called her" (15: 540). When Stephen resists paying the debt of a pound to the Irish poet A. E. in *Ulysses* he argues that he no longer owes anything because his molecules have all changed and a different "I" incurred the debt:

I, I and I. I. (9: 212)

Stephen's alignment of I's allow him to be different subjects at different times, a continuous self from youth to early maturity (I, I) or different selves (I. I.). Each of these configurations, and others,[4] are viable and actionable for Joyce's sense of autobiographical fiction in which the subject is "self-exiled in upon his ego" (*FW*, 184). The sequence of I's also becomes a core issue when Joyce begins to double up on actors in two plots, Dublin's day and Homer's *Odyssey*. Stephen asks about the self what Joyce might about Homeric parallels: "I am another now and yet the same" (l: 311–12). The same question occurs to Bloom: "Or was that I? Or am I now I?" (8: 608).

The reflexivity of *Ulysses* becomes most complex when Joyce approaches in his narrative language the multi-dimensionality of words and syllables that appear later throughout *Finnegans Wake*. When Stephen is very drunk in Nighttown past midnight the text remembers that earlier in the day the discussion had turned to Shakespeare's drunkenness in Elizabethan London. So Shakespeare shows up in "Circe" staggeringly drunk and retching in print over his wretch Iago: "Iagogo! How my Oldfellow chokit his Thursdaymornun. Iagogogo!" (15: 3828–9). Not only has Joyce imitated regurgitation in language, but Iago is Italian for James, and Joyce constructed the Nighttown episode around an incident when he, too, was insultingly drunk on the streets of Dublin on a Thursday night in 1904 (or early next "mornun").

Joyce offers moments of counter-commentary in *Ulysses* when characters unwrite the book that Joyce produces. In the Library episode one of Stephen's foils, John Eglinton, says, "We should not now combine a Norse saga with an excerpt from a novel by George Meredith" (9: 994–5). But Joyce combines a Greek saga with a telegram that Stephen sends to Mulligan, excerpting a passage from Meredith's *Ordeal of Richard Feverel*: "*The sentimentalist is he who would enjoy without incurring the immense debtorship for a thing done*" (9: 550–1). Mulligan says to Haines that Stephen "will never capture Attic note. The note of Swinburne, of all poets, the white death and the ruddy birth" (10: 1073–4). That may be so, but Joyce in *Ulysses* captures both, setting his book on a day in which Paddy Dignam is deposited six feet under at the Glasnevin cemetery and Mina Purefoy gives birth to a bouncing baby boy at the Holles Street maternity ward. Bloom gives his wife Defoe's *Moll Flanders* to read, but Molly tells us, "I dont like books with a Molly in them" (18: 657–8). Joyce certainly wrote one with a Molly in it.[5]

Name Game

A wonderful exercise for reflexively adventurous and spirited readers of *Ulysses* is to imagine alternate titles for the book. Joyce played
the game for *Finnegans Wake* by striking the title from its one definitive place in the manuscript so readers of early drafts would not
discover it before publication – the title became another of Joyce's
gnomons, leaving readers to speculate on other possibilities. Here in
that same vein are some possible titles for *Ulysses* based on the action
in the book or on its links with the epic past. Though phrases are
lifted from the text word for word, they are capitalized as befits titles.

Hellenise It   (1: 158)
Make Room in the Bed   (1: 713)
Usurper   (1: 744)
Ghoststory   (2: 55)
Pretenders: Live Their Lives   (3: 313)
Beware of Imitations   (3: 483)
In the Track of the Sun   (4: 99–100)
Make Hay While the Sun Shines   (4: 173)
Love's Old Sweet Song   (4: 314)
Metempsychosis   (4: 341)
It's Greek: From the Greek   (4: 341)
Seaside Girls   (4: 409)
Useless   (4: 448)
Matchum's Masterstroke   (4: 502)
Dance of the Hours   (4: 526)
Day: Then the Night   (4: 536)
Part Shares and Part Profits   (5: 163)
Good Idea the Latin   (5: 350)
Every Friday Buries a Thursday   (6: 812)
If We Were All Suddenly Somebody Else   (6: 836)
Out of Sight, Out of Mind   (6: 872)
How a Great Daily Organ is Turned Out   (7: 84)
Innuendo of Home Rule   (7: 150)
Who Has the Most Matches?   (7: 463)
Sufficient for the Day   (7: 726)

Links with Bygone Days of Yore   (7: 737)
Pen is Champ   (7: 1034)
Parallax   (8: 110)
Like Old Times   (8: 311)
Irish Times   (8: 323)
Home Rule Sun Rising Up in the Northwest   (8: 473–4)
Me. And Me Now   (8: 917)
What's in a Name?   (9: 901)
One Thinks of Homer   (9: 1165)
What's the Damage?   (10: 325)
Sweets of Sin   (10: 641)
How to Win a Woman's Love   (10: 847)
Strange but True   (10: 978)
Famous Son of a Famous Father   (11: 254)
Real Classical   (11: 280)
My Irish Molly   (11: 512)
All is Lost Now   (11: 629)
Heroes Voyage from Afar   (12: 83)
A Nation Once Again   (12: 917)
A Rank Outsider   (12: 1219)
Christ was a Jew Like Me   (12: 1808–9)
History Repeats Itself   (13: 1093)
Names Change: That's All   (13: 1099-1100)
Good Idea the Repetition   (13: 1123)
Cuckoo   (13: 1289)
Allincluding Most Farraginous Chronicle   (14: 1412)
Harking Back in a Retrospective Arrangement   (15: 442–3)
My Master's Voice   (15: 1247)
New Bloomusalem   (15: 1544)
Long Ago I was a King   (15: 2472)
Dignified Ventriloquy   (15: 3826)
My Experiences in a Cabman's Shelter   (16: 1231)
Domestic Rumpus   (16: 1537)
My Favourite Hero   (17: 644)
Procrastination is the Thief of Time   (17: 644)
The Wonderworker   (17: 1819)

10

Strategic Planning

"Part Shares and Part Profits"

The central event of the day for the Blooms, and arguably the central event of *Ulysses*, is Molly Bloom's afternoon tryst with Blazes Boylan. Readers must come to terms with Molly's infidelity in some way, just as Bloom must. It will not do to pass Molly's afternoon off as Bloom's bad luck – "A dishonoured wife, says the citizen, that's what's the cause of all our misfortunes" (12: 1163–4) – nor will it do merely to welcome Molly's affair as a needed lift – "a woman wants to be embraced 20 times a day almost to make her look young no matter by who so long as to be in love or loved by somebody" (18: 1407–9). Something else is at issue and Joyce goes to great lengths to build an almost subliminal case in the language of *Ulysses* that reveals a sustained reformulation of the fidelity plot in the *Odyssey*. To put it starkly, Bloom is much more involved in the construct of his wife's day than he admits to the reader or even to himself.

The intriguing question for Joyce's readers is whether Molly's adulterous submission does the same thing for the plot of *Ulysses* that Penelope's fidelity does for the *Odyssey*. In other words, does Molly's action actually produce the best chance the Blooms have to sustain their marriage? Even framing the question in such a way seems odd – the notion of serving up adulterous opportunity for sexual stimulation is extreme. Why would Bloom plan his day around his putative demise? There are answers, and they have to do with a well of prudent generosity in Bloom that makes him in Joyce's estimation more heroic than the avenger of the *Odyssey*.

Early in the day Bloom describes Boylan as a "Friend of the family" (4: 440). Bloom could mean "friend" as a euphemism for Molly's lover or "friend" as partner in a scheme to reorient her affections. "Well, it's like a company idea, you see. Part shares and part profits" (8: 784–5), Bloom tells Nosey Flynn in regard to the Belfast concert tour with Molly and Boylan planned for the next week. He uses the corporate "we" when he substitutes the words of a popular song for the night Molly first met Boylan: "Why I bought her the violet garters. Us too: the tie he wore, his lovely socks and turned up trousers. He wore a pair of gaiters the night that first we met. His lovely shirt was shining beneath his what? of jet" (13: 799–802).

At the end of the day we learn of Boylan's "colleagual altruism and amorous egoism" (17: 2174). Bloom does not blame Boylan, relying on the principle of no harm, no foul: "matrimonial violator of the matrimonially violated had not been outraged by the adulterous violator of the adulterously violated" (17: 2197–9). In his extraordinarily tolerant way, Bloom seems to recognize that Molly is more enabled by the afternoon's event than paralyzed or guilt-ridden about it. Bloom does not manufacture his tolerance as a defense so much as activate it as a strategy. The text in "Ithaca" ranks adultery beneath the crimes of "poaching" and "impersonation" (17: 2188–9).

Bloom's life at home has at least reached an impasse, if not a crisis. He takes a chance on the day by accommodating a surrogate lover for Molly almost as a parody of male sexuality. That surrogate will serve as Bloom's only chance to get back in the swim of things himself. Rather than viewing the prospect of Molly's infidelity as the deadening end of a long sexual estrangement in his marriage, Bloom holds out the chance that Molly's day might work to their benefit. What Bloom knows is that Molly has to feel that she can still make choices in her life before she can even reconsider alleviating the habitual patterns into which she and Bloom have fallen. The wish Bloom had for his infant son, Rudy, had he lived, is the same wish he has for Molly: "I could have helped him on in life. I could. Make him independent" (6: 83). Bloom goes so far as to imagine Molly exercising a freedom rarely consigned to women, "the clandestine satisfaction of erotic irritation in masculine brothels" (17: 668).

In reference to husbands who take their sexual pleasure in whatever inebriated state they please with compliant wives, Bloom grasps that Molly is very different, "That's where Molly can knock spots off them" (13: 968). She has a will of her own, and Bloom knows that whatever he wants he has to work around her independence and not against it. Even Molly calls him affectionately, "the great Suggester Don Poldo de la Flora" (18: 1427–8). In "Ithaca" we see how Bloom works.

> What system had proved more effective?
> Indirect suggestion implicating selfinterest.
> Example?
> She disliked umbrella with rain, he liked woman with umbrella, she disliked new hat with rain, he liked woman with new hat, he bought new hat with rain, she carried umbrella with new hat. (17: 703–8)

More to the point, when Bloom indicates Molly's presence to Stephen at the upstairs window of 7 Eccles Street, he does so in a way that resembles his larger strategy for renewal: "With indirect and direct verbal allusions or affirmations: with subdued affection and admiration: with description: with impediment: with suggestion" (17: 1179–81). In a comparable way, Boylan is the bait for a much more considerable enterprise. Molly refers to Bloom in her monologue: "I suppose he thinks Im finished out and laid on the shelf well Im not no nor anything like it" (18: 1021–2). She asserts her own independence stridently, if silently, in letting Bloom in on the nature of the day: "I wish some man or other would take me sometime when hes there and kiss me in his arms" (18: 104–5). As with all of Molly's pronouns, it is not clear whose arms, but she gives Bloom what she thinks he wants in abundance.

> Ill let him know if thats what he wanted that his wife is fucked yes and damn well fucked too up to my neck nearly not by him 5 or 6 times handrunning theres the mark of his spunk on the clean sheet I wouldnt bother to even iron it out that ought to satisfy him if you dont believe me feel my belly unless I made him stand there a put him into me Ive a mind to tell him every scrap and make him do it out in front of me serve him right its all his own fault if I am an adulteress. (18: 1510–16)

If Bloom's plan to get Molly's juices flowing succeeds, the reader might well wonder at what? There are still no guarantees, and Bloom knows that. The comic resources of *Ulysses* play out the day as a set of anagrams on Leopold Bloom's name: "Molldopeloob" and "Bollopedoom" (17: 407–8). Has Molly made a dope or boob of him? Or was he doomed anyway? Or are hope and doom always the ingredients of an adultery plot? If things do not work out, Bloom is even ready to consider separation and divorce, just not yet: "Divorce, not now" (17: 2202). Bloom may have made an earlier decision to implicate himself in or at least accede to Molly's affair, but the day still gnaws at him. The hope it holds out is a muted one: "It wouldn't pan out somehow" (4: 533). What wouldn't pan out? Molly's interest in Boylan or Bloom's hope that Boylan as mediator will reenergize their marriage? Bloom is not entirely sure. "I am a fool perhaps" (13: 1098), he thinks in "Nausicaa." What is clear is that the affair with Boylan has not played out completely. Molly thinks, "I hope hell come on Monday" (18: 332), and she knows "then this day week were to go to Belfast just as well he has to go to Ennis his fathers anniversary" (18: 349–50). Bloom calls his annual trip to his father's gravesite some "private business" (6: 217), as if his wife's tour with Boylan is not private business enough. Molly has a week's license to work both her concert and her love affair.

But it is the future that counts, and Bloom assumes he has one, in part by something so simple and humane as imagining gifts he might buy Molly for "her birthday perhaps. Junejulyaugseptember eighth. Nearly three months off" (8: 628–9). Even on this train of thought he pulls up: "Could buy one of those silk petticoats for Molly, colour of her new garters. Today. Today. Not think" (8: 1061–3). Bloom is not given to self-deception. By September circumstances may have changed entirely and both he and Boylan may be out of the picture: "Forgotten. I too. And one day she with. Leave her: get tired. Suffer then. Snivel. Big spanishy eyes goggling at nothing" (11: 807–8).

Prelude

A phrase from Mozart's *"Là ci darem"* aria on the programme that Boylan plans to bring to Molly that afternoon, *"Voglio e non vorrei"* (4: 327), fairly well sums up Bloom's dilemma on the day of *Ulysses*. He jumbles up the Italian slightly as "I want and wouldn't like," but that is the situation in which Bloom finds himself. He has given the day and its prelude considerable thought, and is even keen on the legal machinery of adultery cases in the period, rambling on about them to Stephen in "Eumaeus." Bloom disparages those who spend time "alleging misconduct with professional golfer or the newest stage favourite instead of being honest and aboveboard about the whole business" (16: 1483–4). In short order, Bloom makes distinctions between the private play of adultery and its public performance,

> it being a case for the two parties themselves unless it ensued that the legitimate husband happened to be a party to it owing to some anonymous letter from the usual boy Jones, who happened to come across them at the crucial moment in a loving position locked in one another's arms, drawing attention to their illicit proceedings and leading up to a domestic rumpus and the erring fair one begging forgiveness of her lord and master upon her knees and promising to sever the connection and not receive his visits any more if only the aggrieved husband would overlook the matter and let bygones be bygones with tears in her eyes though possibly with her tongue in her fair cheek at the same time as quite possibly there were several others. (16: 1532–42)

He then suggests to Stephen that he

> believed and didn't make the smallest bones about saying so either that man or men in the plural were always hanging around on the waiting list about a lady, even supposing she was the best wife in the world and they got on fairly well together for the sake of argument, when, neglecting her duties, she chose to be tired of wedded life and was on for a little flutter in polite debauchery to press their attentions on her with improper intent, the upshot being that her affections centred on another, the cause of many *liaisons* between still attractive married women getting on for fair and forty and younger men, no doubt as several famous cases of feminine infatuation proved up to the hilt. (16: 1543–52)

One might think the infamous Parnell adultery case would pose something of a problem for Bloom, and it would had not his analysis assumed that Kitty O'Shea had feelings for Parnell that Molly does not have for Boylan. Bloom could also console himself on the score that Kitty O'Shea's husband cared little for his wife. It is difficult to read *Ulysses* cover to cover and think Bloom feels himself out of love with Molly. What he ends up doing is pushing the question in the Parnell case to the limits of his own: "Can real love, supposing there happens to be another chap in the case, exist between married folk? Poser" (16: 1385–6). Bloom does not give Stephen a chance to answer the question, sensing that the answer is not in the realm of Stephen's experience.

Molly also harbors strong views on the matter of adultery, and they are not conventional. She recalls seeing a play on the subject and she disdains the typical double standard of her times and long after: "supposed to be a fast play about adultery that idiot in the gallery hissing the woman adulteress he shouted I suppose he went and had a woman in the next lane running round all the back ways after to make up for it" (18: 1118–21). Most wives are chained up because of "their stupid husbands jealousy why cant we all remain friends over it instead of quarrelling" (18: 1392–3).

To reconstruct the events of *Ulysses* on the premise laid down by Molly Bloom requires a careful look at the information provided piecemeal in the book about Bloom's contacts with Boylan. What we learn is that they met over nine months earlier, an "acquaintance initiated in September 1903 in the establishment of George Mesias, merchant tailor and outfitter" (17: 2170–1). At the same time, both Bloom and Molly were concerned that their daughter's sexual maturation – "catamenic hemorrhage, of the female issue of narrator and listener, 15 September 1903" (17: 2287–8) – had put a strain on the ease of their own commerce in and around the house. Bloom pointed Boylan out to Molly at an indeterminate time thereafter in the Dublin Bakery Company and Boylan reminds her of the occasion: "talking about the shape of my foot he noticed at once even before he was introduced when I was in the DBC with Poldy laughing and trying to listen I was waggling my foot we both ordered 2 teas and plain bread and butter I saw him looking with his two old maids of sisters" (18: 247–50).

Molly gains the impression that Bloom has been arranging more than a concert tour with Boylan, encouraging their daughter Milly to take a summer job as part of the plan.

still its the feeling especially now with Milly away such an idea for him to send the girl down there to learn to take photographs on account of his grandfather instead of sending her to Skerrys academy where shed have to learn not like me getting all 1s at school only hed do a thing like that all the same on account of me and Boylan thats why he did it Im certain the way he plots and plans everything out I couldnt turn round with her in the place lately . . . (18: 1003–9)

We hear nothing in the text all day long from Bloom exactly what his relations with Boylan have been during these months, but there is a hint in *Ulysses*, albeit in a chapter where everyone seems to be embellishing the truth or lying, that Bloom and Boylan are much friendlier than Bloom lets on. Stephen's friend Corley appears in "Eumaeus" and with him one of the more puzzling and intriguing moments of the day. It turns out that Corley thinks it possible to ask a favor of Bloom, standing off to the side during his talk with Stephen, because Corley has recognized Bloom: "Who's that with you? I saw him a few times in the Bleeding Horse in Camden street with Boylan, the billsticker" (16: 198–9). Corley is not that reliable and the Bleeding Horse is an uncharacteristic Bloom haunt, but whether Corley gets it right or not is less important than Joyce taking the time to plant such a notion in the book. Stephen reports on the conversation to Bloom, who, as he has done all day long, tries to evade the issue, though he does not exactly deny its accuracy.

—He is down on his luck. He asked me to ask you to ask somebody named Boylan, a billsticker, to give him a job as a sandwichman.
At this intelligence, in which he seemingly evinced little interest, Mr Bloom gazed abstractedly for the space of a half a second or so in the direction of a bucketdredger, rejoicing in the farfamed name of Eblana, moored alongside Customhouse quay and quite possibly out of re-pair, whereupon he observed evasively:
—Everybody gets their own ration of luck, they say. Now you mention it his face was familiar to me. (16: 233–42)

A fortnight before the day of *Ulysses*, matters had heated up. The Glencree dinner dance provided the occasion, and Bloom remembers it in "Lestrygonians."

Wait. The full moon was the night we were Sunday fortnight exactly there is a new moon. Walking down by the Tolka. Not bad for a Fairview moon. She was humming. The young May moon she's beam-

ing, love. He other side of her. Elbow, arm. He. Glowworm's la-amp
is gleaming, love. Touch. Fingers. Asking. Answer. Yes.
Stop. Stop. If it was it was. Must. (8: 587–92)

Bloom here repeats one of Joyce's most important narrative words,
"touch," when he thinks that Molly might have signaled her will-
ingness by a code as old as Ovid's *Art of Love* on the streets of Rome
– the stroke of a finger on a palm. Recalling the same evening earlier
in "Calypso," Bloom mentions Molly's battery of questions: "Is that
Boylan well off? He has money. Why? I noticed he had a good rich
smell off his breath dancing" (4: 529–30). In "Circe" we get a hint
that Bloom seemed to sense what was in store even before the dance:
"Not to lace the wrong eyelet as I did the night of the bazaar dance.
Bad luck. Hook in the wrong tache of her . . . . person you mentioned. That night she met . . . . Now!" (15: 2826–8). Molly tells us
in her monologue: "the last time he came on my bottom when was
it the night Boylan gave my hand a great squeeze going along by the
Tolka" (18: 77–8). Molly has something of an understanding of
Bloom's reaction to Boylan as a kind of stimulus: "because he has
an idea about him and me hes not such a fool" (18: 81). Perhaps
Molly's confidence in her actions during the day indicates a certain
level of complicity with Bloom: "nobody understands his cracked
ideas but me" (18: 1407). That Bloom and Molly might be more in
cahoots than at odds manifests in Bloom's notion that the two of
them could contribute a jointly authored contribution for *Tidbits*
magazine: "Might manage a sketch. By Mr and Mrs L. Bloom. In-
vent a story for some proverb. Which?" (4: 518–19). Which indeed?
The possibilities are inviting: "A bird in the hand is worth two in the
bush," or "Don't put off till tomorrow what you can do today."

"Done. Begin!"

On the morning of June 16 Bloom is fairly subdued about the impending Boylan event, but only on the surface. In point of fact, he
can hardly see a syllable of Boylan's name without thinking about
the visit to Molly in the afternoon. He anticipates it and still feels
terribly anxious about it. His thoughts are deeply woven into the
fabric of the day, but in a desultory and fragmented manner. He

even thinks of the epistolary flirtation he engages with Martha Clifford, who answered an ad in the paper, and his reaction overlaps with his suppressed feelings about his wife and her prospective lover. Does he have any claims to make about anyone's behavior given the double charade that seems to be going on in his life?

> Folly am I writing? Husbands don't. That's marriage does, their wives. Because I'm away from. Suppose. But how? She must. Keep young. If she found out. Card in my high grade ha. No, not tell all. Useless pain.[1] If they don't see. Woman. Sauce for the gander. (11: 874–7)

Joyce rarely makes matters easy in assessing everything that is on Bloom's mind this day. It is part of the book's realism to recognize that even unvoiced thoughts can be defensive and protective. Bloom is known around Dublin as the "prudent member" (12: 211), not only for his Masonic connections but also for his general wariness, and the afternoon's events at his home test his prudence and his tact. When Molly, perhaps feeling Bloom out in her way, asks of the sensational circus novel she has by her bedside, "Is she in love with the first fellow all the time?" (4: 356–7) Bloom plays dumb: "Never read it" (4: 357). If he has to think about Molly's sexuality, he deflects it through daughter Milly's: "Will happen, yes. Prevent. Useless: can't move. Girl's sweet light lips. Will happen too. He felt the flowing qualm spread over him. Useless to move now. Lips kissed, kissing, kissed. Full gluey woman's lips" (4: 447–50).

We get our first glimpse of Boylan's presence when Bloom returns from the pork butcher's around the corner and sees a letter on the hall floor. Bloom represses the name but sees the handwriting: "Bold hand. Mrs Marion" (4: 244–5). A few moments earlier he passed the morning's bread delivery van, thinking of Molly, "Boland's breadvan delivering with trays our daily but she prefers yesterday's loaves" (4: 82–3). "Boland" gets as close as "Bold hand" to Boylan. Molly's preference for yesterday's loaves is very much Bloom's hope in the contest of lovers and husbands. Bloom later remembers the game of charades at Mat Dillon's the night he and Molly met in 1887 and his charade of Rip van Winkle: "Van: breadvan delivering" (13: 1113). He continues, "Then I did Rip van Winkle coming back" (13: 1113–14), leaving a question in his own mind whether his return to 7 Eccles Street that night will nullify or validate him.

Bloom rarely has a complete thought about the outcome of the day, but the text of *Ulysses* does the work for him and for the reader. Early in the morning Bloom reads from the pile of cut papers the pork butcher uses to wrap sold items, "Agendath Netaim: planter's company" (4: 191–2). The circular repeats the promise of the plot when it asks a purchaser to benefit from the fields tilled by another in the Palestinian homeland: just send away to "Bleibtreustrasse" (4: 199) in Berlin, that is, "Stay True Street." In a similar way, the text keeps bringing up the curious activity surrounding the Gold Cup horse race run during the day, and the victory of the outsider, Throwaway. Bloom, in effect, brings about another's victory in supplying a tip to Bantam Lyons by the absurd means of verbal accident: "—I was just going to throw it away, Mr Bloom said" (5: 534). When Bloom thinks about those bits of the confusing circumstances he seems satisfied at the end of the day.

What satisfied him?
To have sustained no positive loss. To have brought a positive gain to others. (17: 351–3)

The hope, of course, is that Molly and Bloom gain more out of the day than Boylan, who seemed so lucky that afternoon. But Boylan bet on the wrong horse, Sceptre, a filly no less, a horse that finished a good show but neither a winner nor a placer. As Molly puts it, "he hasnt such a tremendous amount of spunk in him" (18: 154). Surely, "Poldy has more spunk in him" (18: 168).

Bloom's thinking on the matter of the day is not without an unexpected twist or two. Perhaps the affair with Boylan will aid his marriage, and perhaps his estate: "Why not? Suppose he gave her money. Why not? All a prejudice. She's worth ten, fifteen, more, a pound. What? I think so. All that for nothing. Bold hand: Mrs Marion" (13: 841–3). Pound is net value, but also beef to the heel, the cost per pound for Molly. Should Boylan pay flesh weight for Bloom's authorizing his presence?

Bloom goes nowhere during the day without the afternoon events playing back to him in bits and snippets. Phrases of songs sung at the bar of the Ormond Hotel where he eats dinner during the "Sirens" episode draw him back to his home: "Four o'clock's all's well! Sleep! All is lost now" (11: 1242). Is all well or lost? The fugue in "Sirens" offers up the comic version of Bloom's scheme for the day: "Done. Begin!" (11: 62–3). Even some of the verbal paraphernalia that clutter Bloom's mind provide insight on his hope for his marriage and his life: "Dirty cleans" (4: 481) or "Poisons the only cures" (5: 483). Bloom takes out a picture of Molly later that night to show Stephen in the "Eumaeus" chapter and comments on its condition: "In fact the slight soiling was only an added charm like the case of linen slightly soiled, good as new, much better in fact with the starch out" (16: 1468–70).

The very idea of the adultery plot is complex in *Ulysses* and it keeps turning to Bloom's benefit in a way, if we can read some of the signals. There is an interesting moment in "Circe" when the timepiece signals "Cuckoo" (15: 1133), and the quoits in Molly Bloom's bed jingle to reveal a jury of supposed lovers, none of whom she actually slept with, but the last bearing the moniker, "THE NAMELESS-ONE" (15: 1144). It was Odysseus in the Homeric tale who punned on his own name, *Outis* or Nobody, when taunting the Cyclops. In effect the nameless one at the end of Molly's list of lovers is none other than Bloom, exactly as he would have it in the best of all possible worlds.

As much as Bloom has Boylan on his mind all day, he tries to avoid actually crossing paths with him in Dublin. Molly reaches the same conclusion, rejecting the notion of going out shopping to avoid "the risk of walking into him and ruining the whole thing" (18: 445–6). For much the same reason Bloom steers clear of his flat many hours after he knows Boylan is gone. In "Aeolus" he thinks, "I could go home still: tram: something I forgot. Just to see: before: dressing. No. Here. No" (7: 230–1). Again, in the next episode: "Then about six o'clock I can. Six. Six. Time will be gone then. She" (8: 852–3). Bloom's thoughts are muddled. By that time he (Boylan) will be gone, but will the "time" gone be enough? When Bloom thinks about visiting Milly in Mullingar he might as well be thinking about returning early to his own home: "She mightn't like me to come that way without letting her know. Must be careful about women. Catch them once with their pants down. Never forgive you after" (6: 483–5).

The reason Bloom wanders Dublin all day and most of the night is to give Molly the time she needs to ruminate on the day: "And after: thinking alone" (6: 204). Bloom debates how he might fill his hours

– "Could I go to see *Leah* tonight, I wonder" (6: 185). Later he is
eager to check on Mina Purefoy at the lying-in hospital even though
he barely knows her. And he wanders off with Stephen and the
medicals from the Holles Street Hospital towards Nighttown because
he is not yet ready to go home to 7 Eccles Street.

To Bloom's dismay, though, he runs into Boylan all day long. In
"Hades" Boylan actually crosses the path of the funeral entourage.
Bloom pares his nails trying to avoid eye contact with anyone in the
carriage and wonders, accreting his pronouns, "Is there anything
more in him that they she sees?" (6: 201). Is it women in general
("they") he has in mind, or Molly ("she") specifically? On one occasion Bloom imagines a public urinal as a good place for a venereal
disease ad, and then considers something that obviously has not
crossed his mind until that moment. What if Boylan has a dose of
the clap? Bloom is almost crushed by that notion because disease
would bring harm to Molly, while a love affair – preferably one of
brief duration – might liberate her.

> If he . . . . .?
> O!
> Eh?
> No . . . . . . No.
> No, no. I don't believe it. He wouldn't surely?
> No, no.
> (8: 102–7)

This passage is telling in every way, not the least of which is its
repetition of a resounding "no" six times in three lines, a counterpart to the end of the book and Molly's sequence of "yeses." If Bloom
and Boylan had tacitly or actively conspired in the adultery plot, the
prospect of venereal disease was not part of Boylan's *passe partout*.
Bloom is upset here because he would share moral responsibility in
a way grotesquely different from anything he might have planned
or hoped. License for Boylan is one thing, damage to Molly and
himself another. The "Wandering Rocks" chapter sheds an interesting light on the matter when Boylan tries to hurry the fruit basket
he buys for Molly, "It's for an invalid" (10: 322). He damages her or
invalidates her even before he shows up. And when he readies to
pay the salesgirl – "What's the damage?" (10: 325) – he mirrors
Bloom's anxiety, not just about venereal disease but also about the

entire affair and its repercussions. In "Eumaeus" Bloom thumbs through the evening newspaper headlines and notices another Dublin adultery case: "Lovemaking in Irish, £200 damages" (16: 1240–1). Is damage what Irish lovemaking is all about?

Boylan cuts across Bloom's path at the end of the "Lestrygonian" episode, and Bloom has not quite recovered from the venereal crisis. He escapes Boylan by the skin of his teeth: "No. Didn't see me. After two. Just at the gate. My heart!" (8: 1178–9). Two hours later, Bloom sees Boylan again. He recalls a conversation with Molly from the morning hour completely suppressed in the book but revealed as an almost silent mantra that has obviously been circulating in Bloom's head: "Not yet. At four, she said. Time ever passing" (11: 187–8).[2] Boylan then walks in to the bar of the Ormond Hotel where Bloom sits out of view in the grill: "At four. Has he forgotten. Perhaps a trick. Not come: whet appetite. I couldn't do" (11: 392–3). Bloom seems more upset than relieved when it appears Boylan is late for his afternoon tryst. He could never do such a thing to a woman, especially Molly.

Late at night in the brothel district of the "Circe" episode, Bloom still cannot be sure that Boylan even showed up that afternoon. On his way in he sees a man leaving the Bella Cohen establishment and wonders if Boylan is doubling up on the day, or if, perhaps, he had not visited Molly at all: "If it were he? After? Or because not? Or the double event?" (15: 2706). Now that Bloom has reached the "Circe" chapter, readers can test the subtleties of Bloom's repressed versions of the adultery plot and his complicity in it against the fantastic hallucinations of the episode, which magnify the slightest scrap of character motivation into civic trials and public humiliations. Bloom's hallucinations turn on his small sado-masochistic compulsions, though the chapter makes huge scandals out of minor peccadilloes. During his mock trial for sexual perversion, Mrs. Bellingham charges Bloom with giving her the postcard that we know later from "Ithaca" exists in a far less personal version in the bottom drawer of his bureau at home: "I have it still. It represents a partially nude señorita, frail and lovely (his wife, as he solemnly assured me, taken by him from nature), practising illicit intercourse with a muscular torero, evidently a blackguard" (15: 1066–9).

Of the Boylan adventure the "Circe" chapter is merciless, though readers must understand that Joyce's characters at this point are not directly involved in the wild action of the episode. "What you longed for has come to pass. Henceforth you are unmanned and mine in earnest, a thing under the yoke" (15: 2964–6), says Bella Cohen, wearing the Turkish pants Bloom had imagined for Molly earlier in "Nausicaa." In a hallucination marked "Sins of the Past" Bloom faces the charge: "In five public conveniences he wrote pencilled messages offering his nuptial partner to all strongmembered males" (15: 3034–5). Boylan in the abandon of the chapter comes right out and says that Bloom might want to watch him work: "You can apply your eye to the keyhole and play with yourself while I just go through her a few times" (15: 3788–9).

Another issue on the book's mind, if not dispensed in the realism of the events charted, comes up in "Circe" when Bella Cohen mocks Bloom as cuckold: "Wait for nine months, my lad! Holy ginger, it's kicking and coughing up and down in her guts already! That makes you wild, don't it? Touches the spot?" (15: 3142–4). We learn in the "Penelope" chapter that Molly begins her menstrual cycle that evening after Boylan leaves. So she is not pregnant. But the spot touched may well be Bloom's own desire to have another child, and whether the Boylan adventure was necessary to clear the way. "Circe" raises that thought as well: "To drive me mad! Moll! I forgot! Forgive! Moll . . . . We . . . . Still" (15: 3151).

Nostos

After Nighttown and a wind-down with Stephen at the cabmen's shelter, Bloom finally returns home to Eccles Street. He has forgotten his key in another pair of trousers, and that puts him in much the same position as he has been in all day long: "as a competent keyless citizen he had proceeded energetically from the unknown to the known through the incertitude of the void" (17: 1019–20). Without his key, he jumps over the railing to get in and repeats the strategy that he has followed in one or another form throughout: "crouching in preparation for the impact of the fall" (17: 89). After Stephen's departure Bloom re-enters his flat through the street-level door and hits his head against a walnut sideboard: "a painful sensation was located in consequence of antecedent sensations transmitted and registered" (17: 1277–8). Apparently, Molly elicited

Boylan's strong hand in moving the furniture, which makes Bloom's hallucinatory slip in "Circe" at once amusing and helpful. He confronts Molly, with the "Bold hand" letter of the day in mind: "I can give you . . . I mean as your business menagerer . . Mrs Marion . . . . if you . . . ." (15: 325–6). When Boylan moves the sideboard, the "menagerer" literally rearranges the household. For Bloom the immediate result is the pain, but the pain will subside.

At the end of the episode, as Bloom crawls into his bed, the "Ithaca" narrator repeats the words "his own or not his own" (17: 2115–16) from Shakespeare's play about love triangles, *A Midsummer Night's Dream*. Why has Bloom not worked himself into a frenzy at the prospect of entering a bed just occupied by his wife's lover?

> If he had smiled why would he have smiled?
> To reflect that each one who enters imagines himself to be the first to enter whereas he is always the last term of a preceding series even if the first term of a succeeding one, each imagining himself to be first, last, only and alone whereas he is neither first nor last nor only nor alone in a series originating in and repeated to infinity. (17: 2126–31)

Bloom has more reasons for equanimity: "The preordained frangibility of the hymen" (17: 2212), "the presupposed intangibility of the thing in itself" (17: 2212–13), "the fallaciously inferred debility of the female" (17: 2215–16), "the variations of ethical codes" (17: 2216–17), and "the futility of triumph or protest or vindication: the inanity of extolled virtue: the lethargy of nescient matter: the apathy of the stars" (17: 2224–6). The narrator asks about Bloom's thoughts upon climbing into bed:

> With what antagonistic sentiments were his subsequent reflections affected?
> Envy, jealousy, abnegation, equanimity. (17: 2155)

And in summary:

> Why more abnegation than jealousy, less envy than equanimity?
> From outrage (matrimony) to outrage (adultery) there arose nought but outrage (copulation) yet the matrimonial violator of the matrimonially violated had not been outraged by the adulterous violator of the adulterously violated. (17: 2195–9)

For Joyce the conventional adultery plot too often becomes a revenge story, and it is clear that Joyce's pacifism and Bloom's nature do not operate comfortably in such a venue: "Assassination, never, as two wrongs did not make one right" (17: 2201). Joyce means "right" in the sense of reasonable as well as justified. Revenge is for the savage – at least Bloom sees it that way. He told Stephen in "Eumaeus" that he would never be a party to any such thing,

> off the same bat as those love vendettas of the south, have her or swing for her, when the husband frequently, after some words passed between the two concerning her relations with the other lucky mortal (he having had the pair watched), inflicted fatal injuries on his adored one as a result of an alternative postnuptial *liaison* by plunging his knife into her . . . (16: 1060–5)

Molly and Bloom are on much the same page as far as the physical act of infidelity, Molly thinking: "with all the talk of the world about it people make its only the first time after that its just the ordinary do it and think no more about it" (18: 100–2).[3] Molly's monologue in *Ulysses* is an attempt by a male writer to readjust conventional attitudes towards infidelity through an invented female voice. Joyce and Bloom both need Molly to participate in the redress of habitual imbalance that began with the death of the Blooms' infant child Rudy and continues to the present empty-nest syndrome with Milly gone to Mullingar. It may be the fantasy of a male writer, but in her own boisterous, self-protective, and even occasional braggadocio way Molly comes around to the same conclusion as Blooms that the day of the book provides a revitalizing opportunity.

Molly tells Boylan that her sex life is virtually dead with Bloom, but he is not buying that bill of goods: "its all very well a husband but you cant fool a lover after me telling him we never did anything of course he didnt believe me" (18: 355–6). If Boylan were capable of speaking like the refined Robert in Joyce's play *Exiles*, Joyce might want him to say of Molly to Bloom what Robert says of Bertha to Richard: "And she, too, was trying me; making an experiment with me for your sake!" (61).

The "Penelope" chapter begins with Bloom's request: "Yes because he never did a thing like that before as ask to get his breakfast in bed" (18: 1–2). The request ought to be read alongside a passage from *Finnegans Wake* echoing Bloom's name, "even if Humpty shell fall frumpty times as awkward again in the beardboosoloom of all our grand remonstrancers there'll be iggs for the brekkers come to mournhim, suny side up with care" (12). Bloom reasserts his domestic presence by reversing the first scene in the book when he prepares breakfast for Molly. The first word we hear from Molly Bloom in *Ulysses*, "—Mn" (4: 57), which Bloom interprets as no, balances her last word, "yes." That provides a bare-bones version of the most satisfying plot for the day – no to yes. Joyce told his friend Louis Gillet that in "*Ulysses*, in order to convey the mumbling of a woman falling asleep, I wanted to finish with the faintest word that I could possibly discover. I found the word yes, which is barely pronounced, which implies consent, abandonment, relaxation, the end of all resistance" (*Portraits of the Artist in Exile*, p. 197). Molly's series of yeses at the end of the day are echoed near the end of *Finnegans Wake*, "Oyes! Oyeses! Oyesesyeses!" (604).

The only problem is that *no* and *yes* are equivocal words throughout and Joyce knows it. At their simplest level they answer to the tragic and comic spirit of life and literature, but seeming opposites are not always so, and only the least examined and least complex life projects them as so. We are therefore attuned by the day not to see *no* or *yes* as necessarily excluding each other. And they never do. Blazes Boylan's secretary answers the phone and her brief side of the conversation leaves the day very much in doubt: "Yes, sir. No, sir. Yes, sir" (10: 389). When Bloom in "Circe" feels pressured by the charges against him he replies to a question about his marriage, "Nes Yo" (15: 2766). In "Eumaeus" the lying sailor answers Bloom's question about visiting Gibraltar (Molly's birthplace) with an equivocal, "The sailor grimaced, chewing, in a way that might be read as yes, ay or no" (16: 612–13). In "Ithaca" Bloom describes Molly's "indeterminate response to inaffirmative interrogation" (17: 1163).

About Bloom's request for breakfast – a trial balloon in his mind – Molly is far from over-sentimental. She thinks: "I suppose it was meeting Josie Powell and the funeral and thinking about me and Boylan set him off" (18: 168–70). Her reaction to Bloom's end-of-a-hard-day confidence is a curious one, given that she is the one who has just committed adultery: "Ill just give him one more chance" (18: 1497–8). She knows Bloom very well. In some sense, they have come to an agreement about the day without ever, insofar as we are told in the narrative, actually talking about it. We know some other things about the marriage that Joyce is careful to tell us, although he distributes the information piecemeal over the course of the day. Molly thinks of Boylan's lovemaking, "I noticed the contrast he does it and doesnt talk" (18: 592), the implication being that Bloom does. And what might Bloom talk about? Bloom himself lets us know when he remembers a narrative, if not sexual, encounter with a girl in Meath Street: "All the dirty things I made her say" (13: 868).

Molly's sexual imagination in regard to Bloom complements his in regard to her. She knows that Bloom is given to fantasy projections running to nurses and nuns "like the smutty photo he has shes as much a nun as Im not" (18: 22). We can draw from this little projected vignette that Molly is privy to Bloom's constructed habits of arousal: costumes, role playing, story telling.[4] To the extent that Molly desires she indulges him. Molly's guess that Bloom has ejaculated during the day – "yes he came somewhere" (18: 34) – is an indication that she intuitively knows what her tryst with Boylan means for Bloom. Indeed, a few minutes after he does ejaculate in "Nausicaa" Bloom imagines ejaculating again because his watch seems to have stopped at the moment Molly and Boylan were first occupied.

> Funny my watch stopped at half past four. Dust. Shark liver oil they use to clean. Could do it myself. Save. Was that just when he, she?
> O, he did. Into her. She did. Done.
> Ah! (13: 846–50)

Bloom imagines others have shared time with Molly or space in his bed, but his list, with the exception of Mulvey and Boylan, is pure fantasy.[5] These men are in the Blooms' bedroom because Bloom projected them as lovers, either in his own mind or in conjunction with Molly.

> What preceding series?
> Assuming Mulvey to be the first term of his series, Penrose, Bartell d'Arcy, professor Goodwin, Julius Mastiansky, John Henry Menton, Father Bernard Corrigan, a farmer at the Royal Dublin Society's Horse Show . . . (17: 2132–5)

The list goes on to include the Lord Mayor of Dublin, an organ grinder, Simon Dedalus, and Boylan. For Bloom there is no actual threat from these names, perhaps even Boylan's. Molly knows that her attraction to others arouses Bloom far more than it angers him or even renders him insecure. She recalls an episode in which she surreptitiously kissed the tenor Bartell d'Arcy, whose other appearance was in Joyce's *Dubliners* story, "The Dead": "Ill tell him about that some day not now and surprise him and Ill take him there and show him the very place too we did it so now there you are like it or lump it he thinks nothing can happen without him knowing" (18: 279–82). She may intend to deflate Bloom, but she also knows the story will probably stimulate him, as in the past when Bloom would be

> drawing out the thing by the hour question and answer would you do this that the other with the coalman yes with a bishop yes I would because I told him about some dean or bishop was sitting beside me in the jews temples gardens when I was knitting that woollen thing a stranger to Dublin what place was it and so on about the monuments and he tired me out with statues encouraging him making him worse than he is who is in your mind now tell me who are you thinking of who is it tell me his name who tell me who the german Emperor is yes imagine Im him think of him can you feel him trying to make a whore of me what he never will he ought to give it up now at this age of his life . . . (18: 88–97)

We can glean the same from Joyce's play, *Exiles*. Bertha says to Robert about Richard, "He asks about everything. The ins and outs" (80). This is graphic enough, but Robert wants to know how Richard reacted to his attempt to seduce Bertha. Bertha laughs at this point: "It excited him. More than usual" (81). It is plausible to imagine something similar for *Ulysses*. Molly's famous merging of the many pronoun references in the last chapter of the book, and most especially on its last pages, is testimony to a re-energized sexuality, which, whether Bloom says it, or knows it, or imagines it, is what he may have had in mind all along. When Molly recalls Bloom's proposal on Howth Head she does so with full-throated excitement, and leaves open the option for selecting not just one but all the Penelopean suitors for her own delectation (and Bloom's). Upon that principle Joyce turns infidelity back into loyalty and the spaces of the Dublin epic back to the Mediterranean and to

Gibraltar where I was a Flower of the mountain yes when I put the rose in my hair like the Andalusian girls used or shall I wear a red yes and how he kissed me under the Moorish wall and I thought well as well him as another and then I asked him with my eyes to ask again yes and then he asked me would I yes to say yes my mountain flower and first I put my arms around him yes and drew him down to me so he could feel my breasts all perfume yes and his heart was going like mad and yes I said yes I will Yes. (18: 1602–9)

Notes

Chapter 1: Introducing Joyce

1 When Otto Luening was 95 years old he invited a National Endowment for the Humanities summer seminar on Joyce to his apartment in New York and spoke for hours about Joyce and his time with the English Players theatrical troupe. These remembrances are from that 1995 session.

2 Stanislaus Joyce, *My Brother's Keeper: James Joyce's Early Years* (New York: Viking Press, 1958), p. 105.

3 Joyce told his friend Georges Borach that "Many people think I am a spoiled priest' (*Portraits of the Artist in Exile*, p. 71). And another friend, Robert McAlmon, reports upon hearing Joyce read Dante, "I believed that Joyce might have been a priest upon hearing him recite Dante as though saying mass" (*Interviews and Recollections*, p. 105). Joyce's one recording of *Ulysses* has him reading a passage that, in part, parodies Augustine. He intones the text much as one would imagine a liturgical exercise.

4 *My Brother's Keeper*, pp. 103–4.

5 Friedrich Nietzsche, *On the Genealogy of Morality*, ed. Keith Ansell-Pearson (Cambridge, 1994), p. 71.

Chapter 2: Master Plots

1 See Zack Bowen's *Ulysses as a Comic Novel* (Syracuse: Syracuse University Press, 1989) for a review of the comic properties in Joyce.

2 See the Linati–Gorman–Gilbert schema reprinted in full as an unpaginated Appendix in Richard Ellmann's *Ulysses on the Liffey* (Ox-

ford: New York, 1972).

3   Joyce was fond of saying that Nora made him a man and made him a writer. Bertha Rowan says the same of her husband, the artist Richard Rowan, in Joyce's *Exiles*: "I made him a man" (100).

4   Robert Hand alters the words first articulated by Gabriel for Bertha in Joyce's *Exiles*: "I think of you always – as something beautiful and distant – the moon or some deep music" (32). Joyce is conventional enough in linking woman to the moon and music. He does the same with the soprano Molly Bloom in a long passage in *Ulysses*, responding to the question in "Ithaca," "What special affinities appeared to him to exist between the moon and woman?" (17: 1157–8).

5   A. L. P. is Anna Livia Plurabelle, the pubkeeper's wife in the book.

6   Nabokov speaks beautifully to the matter of lover and wife as muse when he has John Shade write in his poem "Pale Fire" the following lines (*Pale Fire* ([G. P. Putnam's and Sons: New York, 1962], p. 68):

> And all the time, and all the time, my love,
> You too are there, beneath the word, above
> The syllable, to underscore and stress
> The vital rhythm. One heard a woman's dress
> Rustle in the days of yore. I've often caught
> The sound and sense of your approaching thought
> And all in you is youth, and you make new.
> By quoting them, old things I made for you.

7   See Richard Brown's *Joyce and Sexuality* (Cambridge: Cambridge University Press, 1985) for a full discussion of these matters.

8   Frank Budgen, *Myselves When Young* (London: Oxford University Press, 1970), p. 188.

Chapter 3: *Dubliners*

1   The heraldic shield for the city of Dublin pictures twins (it seems) wearing revealing Roman dress and flanking the city's barbicans. Joyce calls the duo in *Finnegans Wake* "*a pair of Sloppy Sluts plainly showing all the Unmentionability*" (107).

2   The Revivalist poet A. E. (George Russell) accepted the first stories, "The Sisters" and "Eveline," for his magazine, *The Irish Homestead*.

3   I. Jackson Cope made this point many years ago in his book *Joyce's Cities: Archaeologies of the Soul* (Baltimore: The Johns Hopkins University Press, 1982).

4   Joyce repeated the phrasing in a different way in 1904, when he wrote a friend, Constantine Curran, that he was working on a "series of epicleti" [the central mystery in the Catholic mass when substance becomes spiritual], called "*Dubliners* to betray the soul of that hemiplegia or paralysis which many consider a city" (*Letters*, I: 55).

5   There is evidence in *Ulysses* that the man who shows up at the funeral in the "Hades" episode is Mr. James Duffy from the story "A Painful Case." But there are other candidates as well. The mystery is intentionally gnomonic.

6   Terence Brown's excellent introduction to the Penguin *Dubliners* makes the point briefly. I have much expanded his observation because it seems to be at the center of so much Joyce does in these stories and in subsequent works.

7   The prose cadences of the end of "The Dead" echo the poetic cadences of the verses Joyce wrote about Nora and Michael Bodkin, "She Weeps over Rahoon" (*James Joyce: Collected Poems* [New York: Viking, 1957], p. 50).

> Rain on Rahoon falls softly, softly falling,
> Where my dark lover lies.
> Sad is his voice that calls me, sadly calling,
> At grey moonrise.

8   That Joyce had something of Nora in mind for "Eveline" becomes clearer in *Finnegans Wake* when Joyce himself appears as Frank, speaking of "taking what he fondly thought was a short cut to Caer Fere, Soak Amerigas, vias the shipsteam *Pridewin*" (171).

9   There are those who think Mr. Duffy is a closeted homosexual at a time when public scandals in Britain around the time of the Oscar Wilde trials made it none too safe to proclaim one's habits and desires. As for Joyce, his politics allow for toleration in all areas, but his Catholicism, even in lapsed form, did not favor trumpeting homosexuality.

10   *My Brother's Keeper*, p. 228.

Chapter 4: *Portrait of the Artist as a Young Man*

1   Richard Ellmann cites the entry in *James Joyce: New and Revised* (New York: Oxford University Press, 1986), p. 147.

2   John Stanislaus Joyce wrote a birthday letter to his son, James, in 1931: "I wonder do you recollect the old days in Brighton Square, when you were Babie Tuckoo, and I used to take you out in the Square and tell

you all about the moo-cow that used to come down from the mountain and take little boys across?" (*Letters*, 3: 212). Apparently John Joyce forgot, or never read, *Portrait*. In any case, Joyce must have been charmed with the remembrance.

3 John Paul Riquelme's excellent book, *Teller and Tale in Joyce's Fiction: Oscillating Perspectives* (Baltimore: Johns Hopkins University Press, 1983), makes the point that the mobius strip is one of the defining features of Joyce's narrative structures. His argument is complex but convincing.
4 Hugh Kenner was the first to make this point with flair and conviction in his *Dublin's Joyce* (London: Chatto and Windus, 1955).
5 In *Stephen Hero* the provenance of the villanelle has an interesting history. Stephen was composing it on Eccles Street when he also formulated his notion of the role of epiphanies in art generally. Later, 7 Eccles Street is not only where Joyce sets the Bloom household in *Ulysses*, but also where friends told him that Nora Barnacle had, indeed, been faithful to him in 1904 before they left for Europe. His friends were not sure, actually, but they told him that to calm his nerves.

Chapter 5: *Exiles*

1 Pound/Joyce: *The Letters of Ezra Pound to James Joyce, with Pound's Essays on Joyce*, ed. Forrest Read (New York: New Directions, 1967), p. 139.
2 Freiherr v. Sacher Masoch is the divorce case in which Sacher Masoch's wife complained of the adulterous liaisons forced on her by her husband.
3 Joyce picks up the phrasing almost word for word from an essay he wrote on "The Shade of Parnell": "The melancholy which invaded his mind was perhaps the profound conviction that, in his hour of need, one of the disciples who dipped his hand in the same bowl with him would betray him" (*CW*, 228).

Chapter 6: Levels of Narration

1 Luening was a young musician studying in Zurich with Joyce's duplex flat mate at the time. His recollections come from an interview in New York, 1995 (see ch. 1, no. 1).
2 David Hayman's term for Joyce's overall control of the narrative in *Ulysses* was "arranger." See his excellent study of a variety of Joycean techniques in *Ulysses, the Mechanics of Meaning*, revised edn. (Madison: University of Wisconsin Press, 1970). For the most elegant and ironic

look at Joyce's manipulation of narrative voices, see Hugh Kenner's *Joyce's Voices* (Berkeley: University of California Press, 1978).

3 Joyce of course hovers in the background thinking about the application of the events of this day to the Homeric *Odyssey*, but that is another mode of narration discussed further along in the chapter.

4 In her recent *Ulysses and the Metamorphoses of Stephen Dedalus* (Lewisburg, PA: Bucknell University Press, 2001), Margaret McBride reveals the immense amount of work Dedalus does as a writer during the day of *Ulysses.*

5 Joyce added the headlines in late revision to the chapter. The first appearance of the episode in serial form in the *Little Review* had no inserted headlines.

6 Michael Groden explains exactly how this process takes place during the many stages of the composition of the book in *Ulysses in Progress* (Princeton: Princeton University Press, 1979).

Chapter 7: Homer in *Ulysses*

1 Earlier on that same evening Joyce narrowly avoided another altercation when he showed up drunk at the Abbey Theatre. Mulligan alludes to the incident in *Ulysses*, introducing the Abbey's most famous playwright, J. Millington Synge, at his home in the process: "—The tramper Synge is looking for you, he said, to murder you. He heard you pissed on his halldoor in Glasthule. He's out in pampooties to murder you" (9: 569–71).

2 See previously cited appendix to Ellmann's *Ulysses on the Liffey.*

3 These logs were themselves adaptations of mythic stories of geographical place names along the coasts of Asia, Africa, and the Mediterranean new lands now called Italy and Spain. Joyce read very carefully the analysis that in his estimation confirmed this reading in Victor Bérard's *Les Phéniciens et l'Odyssée*, and then told his friend Stuart Gilbert to get a grip on Bérard's argument before Gilbert wrote the first important book on understanding *Ulysses*. See Stuart Gilbert, *James Joyce's Ulysses* (Vintage Books: New York, 2nd edn., 1952), p. vii. See also Michael Seidel, *Epic Geography: James Joyce's Ulysses* (Princeton: Princeton University Press, 1975).

4 Bloom seems to track a reverse path for the epic he is in when he thinks about the route traveled by the fruit on display in the shops of Dublin: "Coming all that way: Spain, Gibraltar, Mediterranean, the Levant" (4: 211–12).

5 Joyce in correspondence and conversation named his episodes after the Homeric adventures and tried in each chapter to effect a writing

style appropriate to the theme of that adventure. Karen Lawrence offers the most intricate and extensive argument to this effect in *The Odyssey of Style in Ulysses* (Princeton: Princeton University Press, 1981). As far as the other thing the pen is mightier than, the pun speaks for itself.

6   In *Finnegans Wake*, Anna Livia says to and of her husband, "what wouldn't you give to have a girl! Your wish was mewill" (620).

Chapter 9: Reflexive Fiction

1   The best pure reader of Joyce's immensely innovative phrases and passages is Fritz Senn, *Joyce's Dislocutions: Essays on Reading as Translation* (Baltimore: Johns Hopkins University Press, 1984).

2   The Joyce schema reprinted in Ellmann, *Ulysses on the Liffey*, list the organs, from the kidneys of "Calypso" to the lungs of the wind chapter, "Aeolus," to the brain of the Library chapter, "Scylla and Charybdis." When Joyce is done he builds a complete body for his epic.

3   The Rosenbach facsimile of the *Ulysses* manuscript in Joyce's hand is readily available. See *James Joyce, Ulysses. A Facsimile of the Manuscript*, eds. Harry Levin and Clive Driver, 3 vols. (New York and Philadelphia: Rosenbach Foundation, 1975).

4   Without belaboring the point, the alignments register in different ways depending upon how one interprets the commas, conjunctions, and periods. Each arrangement produces a different take on the status of the subject in autobiographical fiction.

5   Apparently Nora Joyce did not like books with a Molly in them either, especially a Molly based on her. She claimed never to have read *Ulysses*.

Chapter 10: Strategic Planning

1   Joyce seems to know what the Greek mythographers knew in choosing the name Odysseus. The name in Greek is close to the word for trouble, difficulty, travail, *pain*. The scar on Odysseus's leg recognized by the servant at Ithaca late in the epic is said to be a symbol of the hero's name.

2   Margaret McBride first made this point in a brilliant essay, "At four she said," *James Joyce Quarterly*, 17: 1(1979), 21–39.

3   These notions get a reprise in *Finnegans Wake* when we hear that the "pleasures of love lasts but a fleeting but the pledges of life outlusts a lifetime" (444).

4   The Blooms' relationship throws a kind of back light on that of Gabriel
    Conroy and Gretta in "The Dead." When Gabriel mistakenly thinks
    that Gretta feels the same desire for him that he does for her he exults:
    "Moments of their secret life together burst like stars upon his memory"
    (214). He "longed to recall to her those moments, to make her forget
    the years of their dull existence together and remember only their
    moments of ecstasy" (215). Perhaps Michael Furey is one secret Gretta
    would have done well to share with Gabriel before this night in the
    story. Gabriel is devastated not only because of the misdirection of his
    desire, but perhaps because of the occlusion of potential stimulus from
    a dead rival.
5   Bloom does not know about the only other man Molly slept with dur-
    ing the marriage, Lieutenant Gardner, killed in the Boer War.

Index

A. E. *see* Russell, George
Abbey Theatre   72, 150
adamelegy   26
adultery
  adultery plots   38, 75, 78, 127,
    129, 136, 137, 138, 141
  Bloom on   130
  Exiles   38, 73, 75
  Molly on   131
  private play/public performance
    distinction   130
  and revenge   141
  test of free will   73
  Ulysses   38, 75, 78, 127, 129,
    136, 137, 138
"After the Race"   44, 46, 49
Ancient Mariner   67
"Araby"   31–2, 45, 49–50, 52, 71
  Mangan's sister   31–2, 49–50,
    71
Arp, Hans   4
art, erotics of   71
artist
  artistic creation   15–17, 22
  artistic escape   20–1, 24
  the exilic artist   20–1, 22
  as maker and imitator   66–7,
    69–70

Barnacle, Nora *see* Joyce, Nora
Barnes, Djuna   80
Beckett, Samuel   2
betrayal   7, 8, 9, 24
Bloom, Leopold   4, 5–6, 27–8, 38,
    45–6, 90, 97, 98, 102, 111,
    112–14, 119, 121, 126–44
  on adultery   130
  on Boylan   127, 143
  complicity in Molly's adultery
    46, 78, 115, 125, 129, 138
  conversations with Stephen   21,
    83, 110, 111, 130, 132, 136,
    141
  desire for another child   30,
    113, 139
  generosity   126
  habits of arousal   143
  hopes for his marriage   104–5,
    126, 135, 136
  interior narration   94–5, 134
  Jewishness   107, 108
  Joyce on   112
  Joycean qualities   112
  literal and metaphoric desire to
    touch   114
  on marital love   131
  meets Boylan   131

Bloom, Leopold *contd*
  on Milly 136
  and Milly's sexual maturation
    112–13, 131
  on Molly 127–8, 134
  outsider status 107, 112
  pacifism 10, 11, 112
  politics 11
  polytropic qualities 101
  proposes to Molly 35, 71, 96,
    144
  prudence and tact 134
  returns to Eccles Street 139–40
  sado-masochistic compulsions
    138
  son's death 106–7, 112
  tolerance 127
  visits father's grave 129
Bloom, Milly 112–13, 117, 122,
    131–2, 134, 136
Bloom, Molly 30, 31, 99, 114–15,
    119, 123, 128–9
  on adultery 131, 141
  adultery *see* Boylan, Blazes
  on Bloom 108, 128
  Bloom's proposal to 35, 71, 96,
    144
  on Boylan 135, 143
  complicity with Bloom 133
  dislike of books with a "Molly"
    in them 123
  first and last words 115, 137,
    142
  knowledge of Bloom's habits of
    arousal 143, 144
  meets Boylan 131
  merging of pronoun references
    144
  monologue 79, 128, 131–2,
    133, 141
  need to feel desired 114
  and Penelope 37, 105

sexuality 134, 143
"Boarding House, The" 2, 28,
    32, 47, 49, 50, 51
  Bob Doran 51
  Mrs. Mooney 50, 51
  reparation 51
Bodkin, Michael 39, 52, 148
Borach, Georges 23, 100, 146
Boylan, Blazes 78, 96, 108, 114,
    126, 127, 128, 129, 131, 132,
    133, 134, 135, 136, 137–8,
    139, 140, 141, 143
British Navy, Joyce's parody of
    18–19
Bruni, Alessandro Francini 7
Budgen, Frank 38, 72, 101, 121
Busoni, Ferruccio 4

Catholic Church 6, 10, 11–12, 15,
    45, 50, 61
  artists and 16
  Joyce on 6, 11–12
  papal infallibility 11–12
  see also priesthood
Catholic mass 7–8, 16
  Joyce on the mass story 16,
    18–19
classical (Daedalian) art 62
"Clay" 47
Coleridge, Samuel Taylor 67, 103
comic temperament 2, 28–30,
    146
continuity, hope of 30
Cosgrave, Vincent 39
"Counterparts" 49, 50

Daedalus–Icarus myth 24, 60, 62,
    66, 67, 68, 69
Dana (magazine) 59
Dante 42, 100, 102, 146
  Commedia 57
  Inferno 42

"Dead, The"   12, 32–3, 36, 47, 50,
    51–2, 53, 71, 74, 96, 148
  evocative ending   53
  Gabriel Conroy   12, 19, 32, 33,
    36, 47–8, 50, 52, 152
  gnomon   47–8
  Gretta Conroy   32–3, 50, 52,
    152
  Michael Furey   39, 52, 152
  muse and music   32–3, 71
  rivalry   36
  title word   51, 52
Dedalus, Stephen   60–1, 78
  analysis of Shakespeare   23, 26,
    29–30, 35, 37, 39
  artistic escape   20–1
  on betrayal   8
  civic and cultural paranoia
    109–10
  conversations with Bloom   21,
    83, 110, 111, 130, 132, 136,
    141
  drunk in Nighttown   123
  figure of in-betweenness   108–9
  interior narration   86, 87, 88,
    89, 92, 95
  jealousy of Father Moran   36,
    71
  parody of Apostles' creed   18
  Portrait of the Artist as a Young
    Man   2, 8, 15, 16, 20–1, 33–5,
    60–1, 62–6, 67–71
  and priestly ritual   16
  and the priestly vocation   14,
    46, 64–6, 67, 71
  proto-bard   25
  reference to Ulysses   29, 30
  search for a father in Bloom
    104
  self-exile   106
  simoniac   48
  Stephen Hero   15, 16, 17, 20, 36

  tells ghost story   120
  theorizes about art   69–70
  Ulysses   6, 18, 23, 25, 26, 29–30,
    31, 35–6, 37, 41, 44, 60, 61,
    68, 82, 83, 84, 85, 86–7, 88,
    92–3, 95, 97, 99, 103–4, 106,
    108–12, 115, 116, 117,
    118–19, 120, 121–3
  unnerved by hints of
    homosexuality   110–11, 115
  villanelle   70, 71, 149
  voice, locating   60–1, 110
"Drama and Life"   25–6, 76
Dublin and Dubliners, Joyce on
    1, 2, 7, 24, 43
Dubliners   8, 41–58
  gnomon concept   45, 46–8
  inertia/paralysis   19, 24, 42,
    44–5, 49, 54
  Joyce on   1, 17, 43, 48, 148
  narrative enterprise   4, 53–8
  simony   48
  title words   49–53
  see also individual stories
Dumas, Alexandre, The Count of
    Monte Cristo   67

emigration   9–10
Emmett, Robert   98
"Encounter, An"   46, 49
endings   28
English Players   81
epic consciousness   24–8, 57–8
epic geography   27–8, 150
estrangement and reconciliation
    23
"Eveline"   45, 49, 53, 54, 148
exile   12, 19–22, 103, 106
Exiles   21, 36, 37–8, 39, 40, 44, 46,
    72–9, 144
  action of the play   72–4
  adultery plot   38, 73, 75

Exiles contd
  Archie   75, 76
  artist figure   72, 73, 78
  artistic exile   21
  Beatrice   46, 73, 74, 78
  Bertha Rowan   40, 73, 76, 77,
    78, 79, 144, 147
  bourgeois fable   72
  comic action   76
  failure of first production   72
  fidelity and conscience   74
  geometrical relations   75–6
  gnomon   46
  jealousy   40, 72, 74
  Joyce's glosses on   74
  parallels with *Ulysses*   74, 79
  Richard Rowan   36, 37–8, 39,
    40, 72–3, 74, 76–8, 144
  rivalry   36
  Robert Hand   36, 40, 46, 72–3,
    76, 77, 78–9, 144, 147

Faust   100, 101
feminine muse   32–3, 35
fidelity theme   40, 74, 75
Finnegans Wake   6, 16, 17, 18, 20,
    44, 60, 63, 102, 103, 142, 147
  adamelegy   26
  Anna Livia Plurabelle   37, 147,
    151
  Earwicker   46
  exile   21
  feminine muse   33
  French triangle   37
  gnomon   46
  hope of continuity   30
  interior narration   84
  Joyce on   1
  and Joyce's mission   20
  "landescape"   21
  multi-dimensionality of words
    and syllables   123

recapitulation of *Ulysses*'s day
    118
  rivalry   36
  Shem   20, 21, 36, 66
  stylistic layering   56
  Tim Finnegan   29
  title   25, 99–100, 124
  underwear and the artistic
    vocation   66
Flaubert, Gustave   68
  Madame Bovary   68
Fourth Estate   88, 89
fourth-estate narration   88–92

Galvani, Luigi   70
"Gas from a Burner"   8
Gilbert, Stuart   150
Gillet, Louis   142
Gluck, Christoph Wilibald, *Orfeo*   4
gnomon   44, 45–8, 54, 58, 124,
    148
Gogarty, Oliver St. John   42, 87
"Grace"   4, 11–12, 28, 47, 49,
    50–1, 57–8
  epic structure   57–8
  Tom Kernan   4, 51, 57
Gregory, Lady   12, 122
Griffith, Arthur   10

Hathaway, Ann   35
Hoffmeister, Adolf   1, 3, 63
"Holy Office, The"   12, 109
homosexuality   87, 110–11, 148
Hunter, Alfred   100

Ibsen, Henrik   72
Industrial Revolution   9
interior narration   84–8, 92
  Finnegans Wake   84
  Ulysses   54, 84–8, 89
"Ireland: Island of Saints and
    Sages"   7, 9–10, 11, 14, 103

Ireland
  British rule   10
  home rule   10
  Irish sentiment and self-pity   50
  Joyce on   6–11, 13–14, 20,
    24–5, 43, 44–5
  language   12
  national bard   25
  politics   9, 10
  potato famine   9, 10
  triple bondage   10
Irish Revival movement   12–13,
    25, 109, 122
"Ivy Day in the Committee
    Room"   4, 9, 52

Jarnach, Philip   3
jealousy   39, 40, 67, 69, 71, 72,
    74, 75
Jesuits   2, 34
Jews   107
Jonson, Ben   70
joy   29
Joyce, James
  and artistic creation   15–17, 22
  on British rule   10
  on Catholicism   6, 11–12
  comic gift   3, 6
  on drama   76
  on Dublin and Dubliners   1, 2,
    7, 24, 43
  on *Dubliners*   1, 17, 43, 48, 148
  on emigration   9–10
  Eurocentrism   6
  and exile   19–22
  on *Finnegans Wake*   1
  on Griffith   10
  heavy drinking   19, 100, 123,
    150
  on his family and home   42
  on his literary career   1
  on Ireland and the Irish   6–11,

13–14, 20, 24–5, 43, 44–5
and the Irish Revival movement
    12–13, 109
Jesuit schooling   2
journalism   7
lives with Oliver St. John
    Gogarty   42
meets and courts Nora Barnacle
    19, 31, 42
mother's illness and death   41,
    42
and music   3, 4, 32–3
mystical bond with Nora   31, 53
on nationalist ideology   10–11
pacifism and socialism   3, 10,
    11, 112, 141
in Paris   41
on Parnell   8–9
on *Portrait of the Artist as a Young
    Man*   1
and priestly ritual   15–16
and the priestly vocation
    14–16, 146
public lectures   7, 24–5
readers' difficulties with   2
runs a theater company   81
sexuality   3, 39
teaches in Trieste   7, 9, 13
on *Ulysses*   1, 2, 30, 80, 100,
    101–2, 142
in Zurich   3–4
Joyce, John Stanislaus   41, 42,
    148–9
Joyce, Nora   19, 31
  dislike of books with "Molly" in
    them   151
  Joyce suspects of infidelity   39,
    149
  on Joyce's "dirty mind"   39
  Joyce's letters to   19, 31, 39–40,
    42, 52, 53–4
  Joyce's mystical bond with   31, 53

Joyce, Nora *contd*
  Joyce's passion for   39–40
  on Joyce's triangular desire   38
  meets Joyce   19, 42
  and Michael Bodkin   39, 148
  and Vincent Cosgrave   39
Joyce, Stanislaus
  on epic structure of "Grace"
    57
  on genesis of "Portrait"   59
  Joyce's letters from/to   7–8,
    10–11, 12, 16, 32, 42–3, 51

"landescape"   21
language
  Anglo-Irish rhythms   13
  feminine speech patterns   31
Le Cocu Magnifique   72
Lenin, Vladimir Ilyich   4
Linati, Carlo   101
"Little Cloud, A"   44, 50
love
  and the act of writing   33
  Bloom on   131
  marital love   2, 37, 131
  perversion or bartering of   48
  Stephen and   33–4, 35
  triangular desire   37–8
Luening, Otto   3–4, 81, 146, 149

McAlmon, Robert   3, 38–9, 146
Magus, Simon   48
Mangan, James Clarence   25, 31,
  50
Mercanton, Jacques   107
Meredith, George, *Ordeal of Richard
  Feverel*   123
metempsychosis   121
migration of characters between
  books   2
Milton, John, *Paradise Lost*   65–6
mobius strip   60, 149

mock epic   57–8, 81
"Mother, A"   12–13, 28, 49, 50
  Irish Revival politics   12–13
  Kathleen Kearney   13
  Mrs. Kearney   13, 50
Mozart, Wolfgang Amadeus   129
muse and music   32–3

Nabokov, Vladimir   147
narrative enterprise
  adventure with words   2, 3
  Dubliners   4, 53–8
  escape   24
  estrangement and reconciliation
    23
  fourth-estate narration   88–92,
    94–8
  inertia/paralysis   23–4, 42,
    44–5, 54, 74
  interior narration   84–8, 89, 92
  inventive power of Joyce's
    language   3, 4–5
  Joyce's goals   2
  mixed modes of narration   92–8
  nostos (homecoming)   24,
    139–44
  perfection of detail   43–4
  realism   54–5
  sounded narration   83–4
  supplemental narrative   88–92
  third-person narration   81–3,
    85, 86, 92, 95, 96
  Ulysses   80–98
  vowels   6
nationalist ideology   10–11
Newman, John Henry   70
Nietzsche, Friedrich   17
no and *yes*   142
nostos (homecoming)   24, 139–44

Odysseus/Ulysses   29, 101, 136,
  151

Odyssey   40, 89, 97, 102, 103
  fidelity theme   40, 75, 126
  hero's powers of narration   103
  homecoming   24
  Homeric analogues in *Ulysses*
     89, 90, 97, 99–105, 115, 120,
     123
  human renewal   104
  Joyce on   100
  Ulysses as "complete man"   101
O'Shea, Kitty   8, 130
Ovid
  Art of Love   133
  Metamorphoses   62

"Painful Case, A"   28, 47, 49, 52,
     55–7, 78, 111
  James Duffy   19, 55–6, 57, 78,
     111, 148
  Mrs. Sinico   56–7
  narrative experiment   55–6
  stylistic layering   56
papal infallibility   11–12
paralysis/inertia   19, 23–4, 42,
     44–5, 54, 74
Parnell, Charles Stewart   8–9, 52,
     130
Portrait of the Artist as a Young Man
     28, 44, 46, 59–71
  adventure with words   2, 5
  artistic escape   20–1, 24
  Brother Michael   61
  Christmas dinner episode   9
  Cranly   86–7
  Daedalian vocabulary   67
  Daedalus–Icarus myth   62, 66,
     67, 68, 69
  Dante Riordan   9
  Father Arnall   18
  Father Moran   36, 69, 70, 71
  genesis   59
  gnomon   46

  hell-fire sermon   18, 56, 64,
     67
  Joyce on   1
  "moo-cow" myth   59, 60,
     148–9
  Mr. Casey   9
  narrative of the retreat   64
  nature of art   63, 66–7, 69–70
  Parnell and   9
  peasant cottager episode   34
  and the priestly vocation   14,
     16, 64–6
  rivalry   36, 67, 109
  sensation and differentiation
     63–4
  Stephen Dedalus *see* Dedalus,
     Stephen
  title   59, 62
  "training manual"   63
  triangular jealousy   69
  villanelle   35, 69, 70, 71, 149
  workshop   63, 67–8
  writing voice   60–1
Pound, Ezra   74, 112
priesthood
  Joyce on   14–16
  in *Portrait of the Artist as a Young
     Man*   14, 16, 64–6
  in "The Sisters"   14–15
Puccini, Giacomo, *Madame
     Butterfly*   24
punctuation   83–4, 93

redemptive allegory   18
reparation   51
retreat   64
Revelations   90
revival, stories of   28–9
rivalry   36, 40, 67, 109
Romantic (Icarian) art   62
Russell, George (A. E.)   6, 12,
     147

160 Index

Sacher Masoch, Leopold von   74, 149
  Venus in Firs   74
Satan   65–6
satisfaction, as a literary ingredient   29
"Shade of Parnell, The"   8, 149
Shakespeare, William   29–30, 94–5, 121, 122, 123
  A Midsummer Night's Dream   140
  Hamlet   29, 89, 101
  Othello   39
  Richard III   52
  romances   30
  Stephen's analysis of   23, 26, 29–30, 35, 37, 39
  tragedies   29–30
  Troilus and Cressida   99
"She Weeps over Rahoon"   148
Shelley, Percy Bysshe   70
simony   44, 48, 58
Sinn Fein   10
"Sisters, The"   14–15, 42, 44, 46, 49, 52
  Father Flynn   14–15, 43–4, 50, 56
  gnomon   46
  transmission of mystery   14–15
Soupault, Philippe   21
Stephen Hero   3, 15, 16, 17, 19, 20, 22, 29, 33, 36, 45, 48, 55, 62, 103, 149
  classical and Romantic art differentiated   62
  Cranly   33, 86–7
  Lynch   17
  narrative realism   55
  publication   60
  rivalry   36
  satisfaction and joy   29
  simony   48
  spiritual paralysis   45

"Study of Languages, The"   26
stylistic layering   56
Suter, August   2, 38
Synge, J. Millington   150

title words
  Dubliners   49–53
  Finnegans Wake   25, 99–100, 124
  Portrait of the Artist as a Young Man   59, 62
  Ulysses   99, 100, 102
touch   65, 76, 113–14, 133
tragedy and despair   29
triangular relations   37–8, 39, 40, 69, 74, 75–6, 77
Trieste   7, 9, 14
Turpin Hero (ballad)   59–60
"Two Gallants"   32, 46–7, 48, 49, 54, 71
  drop-in realism   54
  muse and music   32, 71
2/em dash, Joyce's use of   83, 84, 93
Tzara, Tristan   4

Ulysses *see* Odysseus/Ulysses
Ulysses   80–145
  adultery plot   38, 75, 78, 127, 129, 136, 137, 138
  "Aeolus" chapter   5, 15, 89, 90, 98, 102, 103, 115, 116, 119, 122, 136
  Buck Mulligan   17, 36, 81, 82, 85, 86, 87, 89, 105, 110, 111, 112, 116–17, 118, 123
  "Chrysostomos"   85
  "Circe" chapter   33, 38, 91–2, 119, 120, 121, 122, 123, 133, 136, 138–9, 140, 142
  commentary on the action   119
  counter-commentary   123

"Cyclops" chapter   11, 15, 18,
   28, 91, 98
drop-in realism   54, 84, 134
encyclopedic fullness   90
ending   19, 38
epic geography   27–8
epic of the human body   30, 90,
   121, 151
"Eumaeus" chapter   10, 110,
   119, 130, 132, 136, 138, 141,
   142
final satisfaction   29
fourth-estate narration   88–92,
   94–8
gnomon   46, 148
"Hades" chapter   5, 104, 137,
   148
Homeric analogues   89, 90, 97,
   99–105, 115, 120, 123
and incidents from earlier
   books   87
interior narration   54, 84–8, 89
irresolute qualities   104–5
"Ithaca" chapter   27, 91, 99,
   104, 107, 112, 118, 119, 122,
   127, 128, 142, 147
Joyce's comments on   1, 2, 30,
   80, 100, 101–2, 142
Joyce's recorded reading of   122
Joyce's schema   101–2
Judeo-Christian ritual acts   118
Leopold Bloom see Bloom,
   Leopold
"Lestrygonians" chapter   5, 113,
   132–3, 138
levels of narration   81
Library chapter   37, 103, 109,
   110, 115, 119, 120, 121, 123
"Lotuseaters" chapter   94
Martha Clifford   106, 112, 134
M'Coy   94, 108
Mina Purefoy   123, 137

mixed modes of narration   92–8
mock epic   81
Molly Bloom see Bloom, Molly
Mr. Deasy   35, 88, 92, 93, 107
multi-dimensionality of words
   and syllables   123
narrative enterprise   80–98
narrative language   4–6
narrative logic   80–1
"Nausicaa" chapter   91, 96, 108,
   129, 143
"Nestor" chapter   44, 92–3, 107,
   119, 120
nostos (homecoming)   24,
   139–44
"Oxen of the Sun" chapter   54,
   83, 91, 108, 119
Paddy Dignam   28, 94, 113, 123
parody of Revelations   90
"Penelope" chapter   103, 139,
   141–2
possible alternate titles   124–5
"Proteus" chapter   97, 119
publication controversy   80
punctuation   83–4, 93
reader's approach to   106, 116
recapitulation of the day   117,
   118
reflexivity   117, 118, 121, 122,
   123
renewal motif   104, 113, 128
rivalry   36
"Scylla and Charybdis" chapter
   18, 91, 118
Simon Dedalus   48
"Sirens" chapter   91, 94, 95, 98,
   135–6
sounded narration   83–4
Stephen Dedalus see Dedalus,
   Stephen
stylistic layering   56
supplemental narrative   88–92

Ulysses contd
  "Telemachus" chapter   81
  textual clues and reading
    prompts   116–20, 121
  third-person narration   81–3,
    85, 86, 95, 96
  title   99, 100, 102
  triangular relation   37, 40
Vincent Lynch   110
"Wandering Rocks" chapter
  137

vampiric kiss   34, 35
villanelle   35, 69, 70, 71, 149
vowels   6

Wilde, Oscar   148
"Work in Progress" *see Finnegans
    Wake*

Yeats, W. B.   12, 33, 122

Zurich   3–4